The ᴄurse

Memories from a Medium's Life

Fiona Roberts

Other books by Fiona Roberts

Ghost of a Smile Memories from a Medium's Life

Voices Memories from a Medium's Life

The Crystal Ball and other Supernatural Stories

A Beard in Nepal

A Beard in Nepal 2 Return to the Village

A Beard in Nepal 3 Travels with the Beard in Nepal, Bhutan and India

www.spanglefish.com/fionaroberts

Contents

Introduction

Welcome to the third book in the series 'Memories from a Medium's Life'.

In the following pages Fiona recounts more fascinating encounters with Spirit people and animals from her readings, from the past, and from friends' experiences.

These true stories and anecdotes are not written in any particular chronological order, and she dips in and out of the past, as well as reproducing material from present day readings and events. The subject matter is equally diverse, and ranges from serious to comical, and from sad to inspiring.

However, please note that what you will **not** find in this book is a list of examples and explanations of the phenomena mentioned in it. You will not discover here what a ghost is, and how it differs from a Spirit person; you will not find an explanation of how, why and when mediumship or clairvoyance occur; and you will not learn why some people occasionally have spontaneous Spirit visions.

That is because all of these things, and many more beside, have already been examined in detail in her previous book, **'Voices'**.

Nevertheless, in the chapters that follow, you will encounter many interesting and diverse facets of the life of a Medium, and will hopefully learn something new and thought provoking about a range of different forms of communication with the Spirit World.

"Death – the last sleep? No, it is the final awakening."
Walter Scott

Chapter One

Barclay

I staggered out of bed in the complete, impenetrable darkness of a chill winter's night, and made my way barefoot and rather unsteadily to where I knew the door should be, sensed, rather than seen, through the dense gloom that filled every corner of the bedroom.

I felt grumpy and out of sorts, cursing this silent, solitary nocturnal trip to the bathroom that had interrupted my much needed sleep.

I grabbed for the door handle, missed and grabbed again, my grasping fingers making contact with the soft cotton folds of a dressing gown hanging on a hook some distance above the handle.

I pulled the door open sharply, irritated by the dressing gown's unwanted attentions as it swung towards me, undoubtedly attempting to hamper my exit from the room.

The soft light from a street lamp outside the house reached in through the landing window at the top of the stairs and partially illuminated my way, dappling the carpet in front of me with patches of colours borrowed from the stained glass pattern on the window. I walked across to the bathroom staring down at my bare feet, zombie-like, bleary eyed, more asleep than awake.

Two minutes later I came out of the bathroom and quietly closed the door behind me. The warm comfort of my bed beckoned, and I yawned and set off back across the landing, heading for sweet dreams again.

I nearly missed him. I was so anxious to get back to my bed that I almost failed to notice the dark figure standing silently unmoving at the top of the stairs.

But I sensed him from the corner of an eye, and jumped in fright. The hairs on the back of my neck moved suddenly as if an icy draught had gently touched them, sending an unwelcome shiver down my spine.

My first, instantaneous and barely grasped thought, was that the man had broken in, that he was a burglar. I opened my mouth to shout for Tod who was asleep in our bedroom, but then realised, with some relief, that I was not looking at an intruder, but at a Spirit person, a somewhat different kind of 'intruder'. I could see the tell-tale glow of a gentle, other world light emanating from the figure.

Caught unawares, my mind blank, I simply stood and stared at him. The young man stared back.

Even in that dim light, and although his face was partly in shadow, I could see that he was handsome, with short neat dark hair, and I had the impression that he was quite tall. He was wearing a biker's distinctive black leather jacket and trousers, and my eyes were drawn to one trouser leg that was ripped most of the way down from top to bottom, causing the heavy plastic knee defender and part of the trouser lining to hang out.

It looked strange, that ripped trouser leg. It was somehow out of place; almost as out of place as this Spirit stranger standing on my landing in the middle of the night. The young man remained perfectly still, hands by his sides, looking towards me.

Although initially clearly discernible, in just a matter of seconds the figure's outline began to waver and become indistinct. I squinted, trying to keep it in view for as long as possible, wondering what this visitor wanted, wondering if I should say something to him. But before I could get my sleep befuddled brain into gear he had vanished back into the Spirit World, leaving me staring through the gloom at the empty space where he had been visible to me for no more than fifteen seconds.

I heard a voice shout something that sounded like 'Barclay' as he left, although it was rather muffled and indistinct, and I could not be completely sure it had been that particular word.

I went back to bed, grateful for the warmth of the heavy duvet that kept the winter night's chill at bay.

But sleep did not come, and I lay awake for a long time, thinking about the young man I had just encountered.

Tod is a biker and has lost several friends in tragic bike accidents over the years. I had no doubt that this visitor was one of them. But I wondered what he had wanted, why he had come. Why had he not spoken? Had I missed something? Had he tried to show me or tell me something, and I had simply not realised? I sighed.

Something about his expression had touched me. He had seemed troubled and deeply sad.

"His name could possibly have been 'Barclay', although I'm really not sure about that," I told Tod the next morning. "I could be completely wrong about the name – I'm guessing at it really. But he was maybe only twenty five or thirty when he died."

"I don't know," Tod said, "I suppose he must have been someone I knew once, although I don't recognise the description. He's probably someone who was killed in a bike accident. But what did he want? Why didn't he say something?"

"I've no idea," I said, "I only saw him for a moment. He gave me a bit of a fright actually, standing there in the dark. But I was half asleep, so I might well have missed something."

"Well, I've certainly never met anyone called Barclay," Tod said, shaking his head, and I had to admit that *I* never had either.

8

The image of the sad young man, with that odd rip in the leg of his leather bikers' trousers, drifted into my thoughts a couple of times over the next few days, and I wondered if he was around me and trying to initiate contact. Was he trying to tell me something? But I didn't see him again, nor hear his voice. And two weeks later I had forgotten about my late night encounter with him, as my life moved on.

Six or eight months later, I opened the front door to my four o'clock reading. It was cold outside in the near dark, and the winter wind pushed past me into the hallway, bringing a chill to everything it touched. I shivered; glad to be wearing a heavy pullover.

I had never met the pleasant young woman who stood on the doorstep, but I didn't need to be psychic to see how very nervous she was. She was all but shaking, and not from the cold.

I showed her into my room and she took her winter jacket off and sat down on the sofa opposite me. I smiled at her.

"You know," I said, hoping to allay most of her fears about the reading, for I assumed that was the cause of her obvious nervousness, "if anything odd happens *I'll* be the first out that door! Follow me if you're fast enough!"

"Sorry," she said, grinning, "I've never had a reading with a Medium before. I'm not quite sure what to expect. So I *am* a bit nervous."

"That's allowed," I told her, "but certainly not necessary!" and we both smiled. The ice seemed to have been broken, and the young woman settled herself more comfortably in the chair, her hands resting in her lap, her nervousness now seemingly under control.

I looked over at my young visitor. She was probably about twenty five years old and pretty, with very shiny, long, straight, dark hair that hung loose around her face. The jeans, pullover, and knee high leather boots that she wore suited her perfectly.

9

The table lamp in the corner of the room shed its warm orange glow across the carpeted space between us, reminding me that I had forgotten to close the curtains. I stood up and did so, consigning the dank, dreary day to the outside where it belonged, and then I sat down and began the reading.

I soon discovered that my visitor's name was Jenny, and that she had quite a number of family and friends in the Spirit World. Her maternal grandmother, who had died when Jenny was a school girl, took the lead in the reading, passing on relevant information, and bringing other people forward to say hello, some of whom Jenny remembered, some she had never met.

I was very much aware of the intensity of my young visitor's gaze upon me, and I knew with certainty that she was waiting for something, or someone, to come forward. She was here for a particular reason.

And then her grandmother told me that there had been a tragedy in Jenny's life, not long ago; a devastating tragedy that still held Jenny in its grip. I waited, wondering what the tragedy had been, wondering if Jenny's grandmother would tell me anything about it, explain it to me.

Eventually, she did.

It seemed that Jenny's husband had died tragically. The young couple had only been married a few months.

As carefully and tactfully as I could, I asked Jenny if this information was correct; had I got it right? She stared at me for a couple of seconds, her expression a mixture of shock and anguish, and then she began to sob.

As the tears ran down her cheeks and she fished in her pocket for a tissue, I heard a man's voice calling, "Jen! Jen!" and I knew this was her husband.

I couldn't see him, but over the next ten minutes I passed on several small pieces of information that he gave me, hoping I was understanding properly what he wanted to say, and interpreting correctly where necessary.

"He's showing me a single red rose," I said. "For me that's symbolic of an upcoming birthday, probably within a couple of weeks, and most probably someone he's particularly close to." I looked across at Jenny.

"Yes," she said, nodding, "it's *my* birthday next week," and her voice broke as she struggled to keep the tears back. "We had plans for it. We were going away for a few days."

"And he's asking if you remember Paddy Mac, or is it Paddy Wack?" I said, "I'm not sure exactly what he's saying I'm afraid."

"*Of course* I remember him," she said quietly, nodding, "Paddy McDermott was one of my husband's best friends, but I don't think *Paddy* was his real name." She smiled. "I think it was a bit of a mickey take, because of the 'McDermott'!"

"I can hear him talking about the birch trees, and the birch wood," I told her, "but I don't know where the trees are, why they're relevant, or what the connection is. He's not saying. Did he maybe live near a wood as a child? Or enjoy visiting one?"

"Birch trees?" Jenny said slowly, looking puzzled, "I don't know what he means I'm afraid. I can't think of *any* trees that he would particularly mention. Certainly none near where we live. No; no woods or forests. How strange."

There was complete silence as we looked at each other for a moment, the pair of us bemused, wondering, and then, in the absence of any further information from the Spirit World regarding trees, birch or otherwise, I continued with the reading.

As time went on I began to see a vague outline of the young man shimmering through the ether, as if projected from somewhere far underwater, undulating and distorted by the movement of the ocean currents over the image.

He was standing alongside Jenny's grandmother. The image grew stronger, clearer in its outline and detail, and I suddenly realised that he was wearing bikers' leathers and

11

holding a crash helmet tucked under his left arm, against his chest.

"Your husband must have been a biker," I said. "He's wearing his leathers here, and he's got his helmet with him."

"Yes," she said, smiling, "he loved riding his bike. He was so proud of it; he kept it clean, polished it, looked after it so well. He went for a ride as often as he could. I went with him sometimes. We were going to France on the bike for my birthday."

Suddenly, right in front of my eyes, I saw a flash of a motorbike crashing off a country road, and ploughing a path of destruction through thick green undergrowth and low, spikey gorse bushes, between the solid trunks of majestic old trees, and then down into a deep ditch. I knew this was how the young man had died.

"Yes," Jenny confirmed when I told her what I had seen, "that was the worst day of my life. It was such a shock. He had always been such a careful rider, and there didn't seem to be a particular cause for the accident. For some reason he just lost control that day."

And then I noticed the trouser leg. I noticed it because the young man moved a step towards me and turned slightly, allowing me a much clearer view of the torn leather trouser and detached plastic knee defender.

"Oh wow!" I said, smiling, "Jenny, I think I've met your husband before," and I told her about my late night encounter with the young man who I had thought at first was an intruder.

"His name isn't Barclay, is it?" I asked her, taking a chance, grinning, fully expecting her to say no.

But she stared at me, eyes wide, "Yes, it is," she said. "Fancy you knowing that! It's such an odd name."

To be honest, I was surprised.

"I wasn't sure it *was* actually his name when I heard it," I explained. "I did wonder if he was talking about a Bank for some reason, but it's so unusual that I remembered it. I've never met anyone else with that particular name."

Jenny laughed. "Yes, he always said he must have been conceived under a birch tree; why else did his mother give him a name that means 'birch wood' or 'birch tree'?"

We stared at each other.

"Of *course*," I said. "That was why he made reference to the birch trees!"

"How stupid am I?" Jenny said shaking her head. "I should have realised what he was talking about! It just didn't occur to me."

Given the circumstances that was perfectly understandable.

Later that day I looked up the name Barclay on the internet – just in case! It does indeed denote a birch wood or birch tree clearing. I was glad about that.

Jenny phoned me a couple of times over the next few months, just to say hello and have a chat, but I have not seen her since that reading.

She had been 'lucky', and had received the proof she needed, the proof she was looking for, at her very first attempt.

She is now confident that her husband is living on in the Spirit World. Life for Jenny here, without her young husband, is somehow easier for her to bear now that she feels sure she will one day be reunited with him.

She does not feel the need to have another reading, and I am fully in agreement with her there. But she does want to try to understand why her husband died so young, where he is now, and what kind of existence he is experiencing. In fact, she feels almost duty bound to discover all she can about life on the 'other side'.

She has also become interested in the wider area of the Paranormal, and spends a lot of her spare time reading books about the mechanics of Spirit communication and the Spirit World. She has also joined a meditation group.

Jenny has found a way to cope with her loss, and to carry on with her life.

"We understand death for the first time when he puts his hand upon one whom we love."
Madame de Stael

Chapter Two

The Search for Proof

Unfortunately, though, there are many sad, bereaved people who live their lives in the desperate hope that someone somewhere will provide them with the ultimate proof that their lost loved ones live on.

Maybe they will receive that proof one day, but maybe they won't.

For there is absolutely no certainty, no guarantee at all in fact, that any Medium will be able to facilitate contact with a particular Spirit, or bring through in a reading that one, small, golden nugget of information which proves to be a revelation, and which proves to them beyond any reasonable doubt that their lost loved one lives on somewhere else, and that they will one day be reunited.

For many people this breakthrough will never come, though they trudge diligently from one reading to the next, and from one Medium or Clairvoyant to another. They may have spent a lifetime firmly believing in the existence of the Spirit World and in the continuation of the human Spirit after physical death, yet still the ultimate proof of that evades them. That incontrovertible proof, given to them by a complete stranger with demonstrably no prior knowledge of the person or their loved ones, is simply not forthcoming.

To make matters worse, they may well have seen friends emotionally overwhelmed by indisputable evidence of survival, as clear and incontestable as crystal, but still *they* wait.

*"**Why**?"* they ask. "Why have I never received enough irrefutable evidence to prove to me that there is life after death? Why have I never had contact from my loved one? If he *is* living on somewhere else I **know** he would attempt to contact me, to reassure me; he **promised** me that he would. So why have I heard nothing from him?"

Sadly, that is an excellent question, and one to which I am afraid there is no single, clear answer. There are some people who have simply never had, and probably never will have, a satisfactory, evidential message or reading.

So what could be stopping or hindering the process of communication? Actually, quite a number of things!

Ask any Medium and they will all say that the quality of a reading, whether good, bad or indifferent, depends ultimately on three things, which are:

The Medium; the 'sitter' (the person who is receiving the reading); and the environment in which the reading takes place.

A rather simplistic list, perhaps, but it is probably easy to understand that if the Medium is feeling ill, stressed, or particularly tired during the reading, then the enormous amount of concentration and energy needed to facilitate Spirit communication will most definitely be lacking. As a consequence, the reading may be slow, inaccurate, inarticulate or otherwise flawed in some way.

Equally, if the sitter is not well, or is unable to concentrate for some reason on what the Medium is telling them, or perhaps does not fully understand what is going on, or what is required of them, then the reading will collapse.

A sitter, leaning toward the side of non-belief in psychic matters, who attends for a reading anyway, but with a 'prove it to me' attitude written all over them, may sit in front of the Medium, and without due thought or consideration say a very quick and curt, "No!" to something, or a number of things, that the Medium tells them, will thereby have ruined and curtailed their own reading. The Medium will consequently be unable to communicate, or produce any meaningful evidence of survival for that person. It is as if they have built a brick wall between themselves and any possible communication from the Spirit World.

Unfortunately this is probably a good example of a self-fulfilling prophecy i.e. the sitter does not expect to receive any significant information from the Medium, and sadly, largely due to their own negative attitude, they will probably not have an acceptable reading, and will go home with their initial negative assessment of a Medium's ability considerably reinforced.

And of course both Medium and sitter need to feel comfortable, warm and at ease in the environment. Background noise can be a particular problem, maybe the sporadic barking of a dog, or music emanating from a neighbour's house, even heavy rainfall outside against the window, all of which can lead to broken concentration, frayed nerves, and an unsatisfactory or abandoned reading.

The conditions listed above are pretty obvious, but there are *many* other, more obscure conditions which will most certainly interfere with the accuracy of a reading, or even dictate if the reading can take place at all.

As soon as the Medium begins to work and their psychic senses come into play, a number of things about the sitter will become obvious to them, whether they like it or not.

For example, the Medium will know immediately if they actually like or dislike the sitter. They will 'feel' it, and this may well interfere with their ability to give a good, evidential reading, or in some cases any reading at all.

They will probably also become aware of whether the sitter is honest or is in some way trying to deceive; and most importantly, the Medium's psychic senses will alert him or her to the fact that the sitter may actually harbour feelings of hostility towards them.

A strongly held thought, either negative or positive, can often be sensed, even seen, by a Medium or psychic.

17

So, the Medium will very quickly have a good idea of how the reading will go; whether it will be sufficiently evidential, whether the communication will flow or stutter, thereby causing the Medium to flounder, as if wading blindly through thick mud. Yes, I've been there a few times!

Dealing with and sorting out these initial, and sometimes overwhelming feelings and impressions, is not always easy for the Medium as they attempt to get the reading underway.

Most people would assume that if someone goes to a Medium for a reading they perhaps do not know *exactly* what to expect from that reading, because all Mediums work differently, but at the very *least* that person would know what a Medium does or should do, as opposed to, say, a Tarot reader.

But in that assumption 'most people' would be wrong, because there is a great deal of misinformation round and about on the subject of mediumship, leading to some bizarre and even completely inappropriate ideas about the work that a Medium does.

I would hazard a guess that perhaps fifty percent of the population of the UK have never come into contact with one, and do not know, or care, what a Medium does. And of course, why should they?

I opened the door one day to an elderly lady who I had never seen before. Her nephew, who I did not know either, had made the appointment and brought her along for a reading, and he helped her now up the step and into the house. She was quite unsteady on her feet and walked slowly with the help of a stick.

I remember feeling rather apprehensive that she would have to walk through the house, out into the garden at the back, and then up the step into Todington Lodge where I did my readings.

My husband Tod had built the lovely wooden hut for me, and our friends had named it after him. One particularly enterprising and artistic friend had even given us a lovely hand- made name plaque with 'Todington Lodge' on it. It hung proudly over the door.

It was a substantial, attractive little building, and quite a talking point. It looked rather like a Swiss chalet. There was a small pond beside it, home to any number of frogs, and the garden was always full of a variety of birds, many of which enjoyed sitting on the Lodge roof. It was a wonderful, peaceful place to relax or to do readings in during the summer. It smelled pleasantly of fresh, new wood and cut grass.

My elderly client managed the step up into the Lodge and settled herself in the armchair there. She looked around, nodded, and smiled at me.

"Right," I said, smiling back at her, "Are you comfortable in that chair?"

"Yes dear," she said, "I'm fine thank you."

She had an agreeable, gentle voice that age had added a slight wobble to. The sunshine that lit the inside of the Lodge that day glinted off her short, silver-grey hair, accentuating its waves. I wondered if she had been to the hairdresser's especially for this reading. I thought she was probably rather more than eighty, this calm, elegant, well dressed lady.

I began the reading and became aware almost immediately of a man standing next to my client, looking over at me. He was rather short, with dark hair brushed back from his face, and surprisingly long sideburns. He seemed to belong to a bygone age, dressed as he was in what appeared to be dark, Victorian style clothing. I had the distinct impression that he disapproved of what I was doing. His expression was rather severe, and he did not attempt to communicate, but simply stared at me in silence.

I started to try to describe this man to the elderly lady sitting opposite me. She immediately leant slightly towards me, resting both her hands on the walking stick which she had laid across her knees, and looking intently at me.

She said nothing, and neither nodded nor shook her head, but her expression told me she was listening and concentrating hard on what I said.

The man held out his right hand so I could see a large, gold signet ring on one of the fingers. I could not make out the initials on the ring, but I told my client what he had done, and described the ring as best I could, as the man obviously felt that this move would facilitate her recognition of him. But she simply stared at me, her expression unchanged, and yet again said nothing.

I had the sudden fleeting thought that it was unusual, even odd, for any client to remain silent at this juncture. I would have expected *some* response, even if just a simple 'yes' or 'no'.

Then the man turned slightly and I realised that someone else had joined him. The newcomer was a considerably younger man, and I was sure it was his son. The younger man's form was blurred and indistinct, but despite that I could see that he was wearing some kind of uniform, possibly an army uniform, but I couldn't be certain of that. However, he had one arm in an old fashioned looking sling, pulled quite high across his chest. It looked almost comical, as if far too much material had been used to make it, and an uneven triangle of linen hung down at the elbow.

Neither of the men had communicated, so I just had to describe them to my client as best I could, from what I could make out.

"The younger man actually has a *medal* hanging from the sling," I said, smiling. "That looks a bit odd, to say the least! Do you know," I said, looking over at the elderly lady, "I think this is your father, and a brother of yours with him. I'm hoping one of them at least will speak and pass some information on to you."

And I smiled at her again, suddenly wondering why there was still no response from the lady. She had not moved. She remained leaning forward slightly, and her hands still rested, unmoving, on her walking stick. There was complete silence in the Lodge, and I became aware of birdsong nearby, outside the window.

Mentally I tried to shake off the growing feeling of worry that threatened to fatally interrupt my concentration, and I took a deep breath, ready to continue the reading.

Suddenly the elderly lady said, "Thank you dear. That's enough now," in a tone which, while not in any way curt or nasty, spoke distinctly of finality, rather like a school teacher ending a lesson. She slowly pushed herself upright from the chair, clutching her walking stick in one hand, and turning unsteadily towards the door.

It was my turn to stare. I wondered what was going on.

"Is there something wrong? Are you ill? Can I help?" I asked her, getting up myself and moving forward to take her arm and steady her.

"No, I'm not ill," she said, "but this is not for me. It's all very strange indeed. I'll go home now, thank you." And she began to walk towards the door. I hurried to help her down the step outside, afraid she might slip, wondering what on earth I had done wrong.

We walked slowly, and in silence together across the garden and into the house. I couldn't think of anything sensible to say, and decided that my best bet was probably to remain silent.

The lady's nephew looked shocked as we arrived at the lounge door where he was sitting reading a book. He stood up quickly, gathering his coat and belongings together.

"You were very quick," he said, glancing first at me, then at his aunt. "Is something wrong?" he asked.

"No dear," the elderly lady told him, "not really. Only.... Fiona has just described my father – I recognised his description and the signet ring he always wore – and then she

21

described my brother Sam. Of course that's *your* father. I'm quite sure it was them; yes, quite sure." And she nodded her head, her expression serious. I stood in silence wondering what was coming next.

"But of course," she continued, staring straight at me, "we **know** that just can't be so, because they are both dead."

And having dropped that bombshell she turned to walk down the hallway towards the front door.

The lady's nephew and I exchanged glances as he hurried to take her arm. I suppressed what was probably an entirely inappropriate urge to giggle, and instead stepped in front of the two of them and opened the door as they left.

As he walked past me on his way out the nephew mouthed the word, "Sorry!" in my direction.

I smiled. He didn't need to be.

The shy young man who came for a reading one sun bright, blustery day in May told me his name was Anthony. He followed me out into the garden and up the step into Todington Lodge, where he settled himself in an armchair.

I suppose he must have been around the age of twenty five, although with his mid length blondish hair windblown and framing his youthful face, he could have been mistaken for someone much younger.

The signs of the nervousness he was feeling were all there; one foot tapping on the floor, the fingers of one hand pulling constantly at the corner of his jacket pocket. So I spent a few minutes chatting to him generally, trying to put him at his ease.

Then I said, "You don't need to worry about the reading, it's...." but I got no further with my explanation as he interrupted me.

"I know all about readings and how they work – you don't need to explain. I'm not worried," and he stared at me with a weird, almost defiant expression on his face.

"OK. We'll get started then," I said, feeling slightly miffed by his rather strange attitude. But nervousness and fear of the unknown can have an odd effect on people, and I had no idea what was going on in his mind at that moment.

The reading got underway, and I particularly remember two of the young man's grandparents communicating, and passing on bits and pieces of information. At one point I looked up, towards the young man, expecting some kind of acknowledgement from him, maybe a nod of the head, a 'yes', or a 'no'. But instead I was surprised to see him sitting unmoving, staring wide eyed over my shoulder at the wooden wall of the Lodge behind me.

I wondered what was wrong, what he was staring at, but decided it was probably best if I just continued with the reading, and said nothing.

I tried to do so, but began to feel awkward and uncomfortable, and little by little my concentration waned.

Suddenly he said, "What are you *doing*?" in a voice loud enough to be heard in the next garden.

I looked up, startled, "I'm trying to continue with your reading," I said as calmly as I could. "Is something wrong?"

"Of course it's wrong!" he said, his voice lower now, but trembling with emotion, "It's *completely* wrong. As usual! You Mediums are all the same. You don't do what you're *supposed* to do!" And he positively glared at me.

"Well, actually," I said, "I *am* doing what a Medium is supposed to do. So, what is it that you think I *should* be doing?"

"You should be *communicating*!" he almost shouted at me, "'They' should be *here*! And *I* should be able to *see* them!"

"But.... why do you think you should be able to see them?" I asked him, "Do you usually see Spirit people?"

"No I don't!" he said, "But that's what I'm *here* for! *You* are supposed to show them to me!" And he pointed an accusatory finger at me, his expression none too agreeable, to say the least.

"Look," I said, "I'm sorry, but that's not how it works; that's not what a Medium does."

"You *all* say that," he said dismissively, and stood up suddenly.

"We *all* say that because it's *true*," I said, feeling ever so slightly threatened by this strange young man's behaviour. "A Medium communicates, but they *cannot* show you the Spirit person they are communicating with."

"You're wrong!" he said, and turned and stormed out of the Lodge. I hurried after him and caught him up at the front door.

"You Mediums are all pathetic!" he said, and there was a definite note of menace in his voice now, "You want to keep those Spirit people for yourselves and not let anyone else see them!" And he reached out and pulled the door sharply open.

I judged it wise not to respond in any way to these very odd accusations about the work and motivation of Mediums, and simply held the door open for him as he pushed his way past me.

He paused on the doorstep, looked back at me and said, "You're not a real Medium. Any real Medium would be able to show me Spirit people!" And he rushed off down the path and out the garden gate, his hair blowing around his face, giving him the look of a slightly eccentric school teacher from the 1940s.

I breathed a sigh of relief to see him go.

"Where did he get that idea from?" Tod asked me later when I explained what had happened.

"He could have picked it up from any number of books or publications, meeting places, or people. There are some very odd ideas around these days," I said. "But I suspect he's rearranged bits and pieces of information in his own mind, put them into his own particular jigsaw design, and reached some bizarre conclusions in doing so. The bottom line is probably that he *wants* to see Spirit people, and to communicate with them himself, but hasn't been able to, so he's doing the rounds of all the Mediums he can find, and blaming us."

"I do not want the peace which passeth understanding – I want the understanding which bringeth peace."
Helen Keller

Chapter Three

Evidence

I am nothing special as a Medium but I am, and have always been, particularly interested in the mechanics of mediumship i.e. how it works, and why it works.

There are many people, all over the UK, whose mediumistic abilities far outstrip my own rather average ability, and who take Spiritualist Church services, or give Evenings of Clairvoyance, and regularly provide good, detailed, often irrefutable evidence of the survival of the human Spirit after death. And that, after all, is what a Medium should do.

Those instances in which I have been able to receive and pass on sufficiently clear evidence of survival, or in some way to help dispel the cloud of depression or fear around a person regarding the fate of their lost loved one, have mostly hinged on just one small thing, one small golden 'nugget' of evidence.

That nugget may perhaps have been an unusual and therefore memorable name called out from the Spirit World; or a glimpse of an odd or comical situation which, when explained, meant a great deal to the person I was speaking to; or a clear enough sighting of a Spirit entity which enabled me to describe it in enough detail to facilitate sure and certain recognition.

Most of these pieces of evidence do not provide me with the opportunity to construct some kind of explanatory story around them, in order to present them to you in a perhaps more interesting format. That is because they are short and sweet, there *was* no story around most of them, either before or after the event, and they cannot therefore be presented in any other way.

So what follows is, in part, little more than a list of some of my more notable and memorable bits of evidence from private readings.

Last summer Jean, a Scottish lady on holiday in England, came to see me for a private reading.

We settled ourselves in the Lodge in the garden, and giggled about the tiny frogs that were running riot through the grass around us. Most of them were 'new' that year, and were no bigger than your thumb nail. They had been born in the garden pond and were now bravely setting off to see what kind of world they had joined. Each blade of grass posed a problem as it barred their route, and stood considerably taller than they did but, undaunted, those mini chaps tackled everything in their way, climbing to the top of the thin green stems, wrapping their arms around them, and swaying about there in the sunshine.

We started the reading and I remember several members of Jean's family putting in appearances, and passing on bits and pieces of information. But one man stood quietly in the background. I saw him as little more than a dark shadow standing behind her, waiting. He had something in particular to say, and wanted to be heard and clearly recognised.

Eventually he stepped forward and said, "I'm not Mac. Tell her, I'm not Mac."

"I'm hoping this will mean something to you," I said to Jean. "There's a man here who wants to tell you he is, *'not Mac'*. I don't know how he's spelling that, and I assume it's his name, but...." I stopped, waiting, looking across at Jean, wondering what her response would be to this rather odd piece of information.

27

She was smiling broadly, "I know exactly what he means," she said. "He's my father, and when he was born *his* father went along to register the birth. But my grandfather was so excited to finally have the son that he had been waiting for, that he didn't pay much attention to what the Registrar was writing on the birth certificate. So instead of **McPhearson**, the Registrar wrote **MacPhearson**. There was a bit of a fuss when the mistake was discovered, to say the least! Mum was quite annoyed, but eventually it became a family joke! Whenever it was mentioned Dad always said, *"I'm not Mac,"* and of course we kids all found it really funny."

I was doing a reading for a lady one day when I 'saw' a view of a street that I recognised. In the past there had been a very well-known sausage making factory on that street, with a large sign in the shape of a cartoon-type pig, high up on the front of it, carrying a sausage on a fork over his shoulder.

I could 'see' the pig, so I knew which street it was, but I had no other information to give to the lady.

"Oh yes," she said when I told her, "I grew up there. I remember the area well."

"I can hear a man's voice talking about the street," I said. "He's got some kind of quite unusual accent. He's certainly not local to the area," and I paused, wondering if that meant anything to the lady sitting opposite me.

She shook her head slowly, thinking. "Sorry," she said, "I don't know who that could be."

"Oh," I said, "Wait a moment. He's *Dutch*! He says he and his wife ran a chippy on that street many years ago."

"Yes! Yes of course," she said, and her face lit up, "I was just a child at the time but I remember them well. They were a lovely couple."

"He's just here to say hello to you," I said. "No more than that."

A lady from the Republic of Ireland came to see me one day. She was very chatty, and very amusing. It was all I could do to get the reading underway because she wanted to natter, and ask a stream of questions. She had never had a reading before, and was curious as to how it all 'worked'.

I finally managed to get a word in edgeways, and told her that an Uncle of hers was there to speak to her.

"His name sounds like 'Danny' or 'Donny', but he's shaking his head, so I know I haven't got it right," I told her. "He's saying Uncle Donny – no, sorry, it's *not* that," I said, "I just can't make out what he's saying, I'm afraid. Sorry."

The reading ran late, and the lady had to leave quickly afterwards to attend an appointment, so we had no time to discuss the information that had come out. But she had taken careful and copious notes, and texted me the next day to explain one or two things, and to tell me that her Uncle's name was 'Donal'.

I have never been interested in telling people that, for example, "The Spirit World is giving you a big bouquet of flowers," or, "You have the colour pink all around you."

However, Mediums do work with symbolism, and a red rose is, to me, symbolic of a birthday. I may see a single red rose 'handed' to a client, or placed on the table in front of them, telling me that their birthday would probably be within a couple of weeks either side of the date of the reading, or sometimes that very day.

But the red rose may signify someone else's birthday, in which case I would hope to hear or see a name, to put me on the right track.

A tall red rose standing alone in the ground tells me that we are speaking about the anniversary of a death, and similarly, a pink rose would tell me that we are looking at a wedding anniversary.

I sometimes see a date next to the rose, or hear a voice telling me a date. But there *are* grounds here for confusion of course, and occasionally I have been spectacularly wrong, managing to mix up people, dates and anniversaries!

The pleasant young woman who came to see me in June last year told me her name was Anne. We settled into the chairs in the Lodge and I began the reading. There was nothing special, certainly nothing unusual about it, until someone in the Spirit World shouted, "Happy Birthday!" and threw a red rose onto the table in front of Anne.

I opened my mouth to tell her that her birthday had been remembered, but before I could say a word there was another shout of, "Happy Birthday!" from the Spirit World, and another red rose was thrown onto the table to join the one that was already there.

I stared at the roses and wondered if this was two different people in the Spirit World remembering Anne's birthday, or could there by any chance be *another* birthday around this time too. I dithered, and decided to ask her.

"Someone is wishing you a happy birthday," I said, and then paused as yet another red rose joined those already on the table, and someone shouted, "Happy Birthday!"

"Ah," I said, "There seem to be a lot of people remembering your birthday; at least, *I think* it's *your* birthday, or it could actually be three separate birthdays." I looked across at her, "I haven't got a particular date yet," I said, "but someone has written '*June*' here, so it must be this month."

Anne was smiling. She nodded. "Yes, June," she said.

I took a deep breath, ready to continue the reading, but before I could do so a further four roses were placed on the table in front of my client, "Oh dear!" I said, "I don't know if someone is having a bit of a joke here at my expense, but there are now *seven* roses in front of you! I don't suppose you know of seven birthdays this month, do you?" and I laughed, fully expecting her to say *no*, she didn't know of seven birthdays in June.

30

But to my surprise Anne said, "Yes! My close family, and myself, were all born in June!" She smiled, "So yes, there *are* seven birthdays in June. How lovely that they've all been remembered."

How lovely indeed.

I had never met the woman who sat opposite me on the very edge of the chair, clutching a handkerchief in both her hands. Her obvious distress at the recent loss of her mother touched me deeply, and my heart went out to her.

I prayed that her mother would be able to communicate, to bring some comfort to her grieving daughter. Eventually she did.

"I'm afraid I can't see your mother," I told her, "but I can hear her talking to you, and I know it's her. She has a lovely soft voice. She's saying, 'It's for *you*. Keep it. It's for *you*.'" I said.

The woman stared at me but said nothing, so I didn't know if her mother's words meant anything at all to her.

Suddenly a woman's hand, nebulous and ill defined, but just about recognisable as a woman's hand, reached out and placed something on the small table between us.

"It's for *you*," the same soft and gentle voice repeated. "For you."

"Your mother has put a ring on the table," I said, "and she's repeating that it is for *you*."

"Are you sure that she doesn't want me to give it to someone else?" the woman asked quickly.

"Yes, absolutely sure," I said. "She's very clear that it's for *you*."

"Do you know what kind of ring it is?" she asked me.

"I only know that one of the stones is red," I told her, "I'm sorry I can't be more specific than that."

"My mother left me a beautiful, old, ornate lamp," the woman told me, leaning forward slightly as if to emphasise her words, "She had always said that she wanted me to have

31

it, so it wasn't a surprise when my sister phoned and told me. I picked it up from Mum's bungalow, and took it home. I didn't really look at it for a few days as I was so upset at losing Mum. But then I decided to give it a bit of a clean, and I dusted it and turned it carefully upside down to see if it needed cleaning there too. And I saw a ring, hooked on to one of the ornate brass designs underneath. I recognised it as one of Mum's dress rings; the one with the red stone.

I don't have any children, and she had left most of her jewellery – she didn't have much – to her only granddaughter, so I wondered if I should pass this ring on to her too. You see, at first I thought it had got there by accident, but then when I really thought about it that didn't seem possible somehow. How could a ring get accidentally hooked underneath a lamp?"

"I don't think it got there by accident," I said, "I think your Mum definitely wanted you to have it. I think she put it there for you to find. And you did! She has said to you, several times, 'It's for you', and so I think you should accept it, and keep it."

One Thursday morning, not so long ago, I woke up to the sound of someone from the Spirit World saying quietly, "Belle's coming over." I didn't recognise the voice.

The only 'Belle' I knew was my friend's mother, who had been suffering from dementia for a number of years. I told Tod.

"I think Wilma's Mum is going over soon," I said, "Probably tomorrow."

But she died on the Saturday.

I was in the middle of a reading, concentrating on passing on the information as best I could, when I noticed, out of the corner of my eye, a large dog walk slowly in through the door of the Lodge. Its form was unclear, wavering through the ether, as if I was seeing it at a distance, under the ocean, with the currents ebbing and flowing over it, shredding its outline, turning it into a nebulous spectre. But as I turned my attention to the dog its outline became clearer, and I saw that it was a large, elderly golden Labrador, with a lovely face and dark, shining, expressive eyes.

And then someone called out from the Spirit World, "This is 'Lady'; our beautiful 'Lady'."

I felt very emotional, and knew that this was a much loved dog that someone had just lost.

"Yes," the woman sitting opposite me said, "That's Lady, my sister's golden Labrador. She died a week ago."

Our friend Patty lives in the south of England, so it is always nice when she comes north to visit us, and we can spend time together catching up on all the news.

During her visit a couple of years ago we went to a country pub for lunch. Tod and I knew the pub and had eaten there before, so we knew it would be very quiet at lunchtime in the middle of the week. Sure enough when we got there the pub was almost empty, with just a couple of people talking together at the bar. We sat down at a table in one of the empty dining rooms.

The pub has been there since the 1700s, and although it has been renovated over the years it still retains the oak beams and traditional style that make it so attractive to its modern day visitors.

Having ordered, we chatted while we waited for our meals to arrive, and Patty began explaining something or other to Tod. I was only half listening, and my mind wandered as I glanced around the room.

Although I hadn't seen him come in, an elderly man had seated himself at a small table by the door. He was wearing an old tweed jacket and had a tweed cap on – a tuft of grey hair protruded from under it at the back. The thought that he was a farmer drifted into my mind, and out again. I looked away, and returned my attention to what Patty and Tod were saying.

A matter of seconds later the sudden loud noise of something being dropped in the area of the bar made all three of us turn and look in that direction, and I jumped with shock as I realised that the 'farmer' had gone. He was no longer visible to me, and I realised that he had in fact been a Spirit person.

"What's up?" Tod and Patty asked me.

I explained what I had seen, and we spent some time discussing spontaneous Spirit sightings*, of which this was one, concluding finally that the elderly man may well have been a regular at the pub, many years before.

*For a full explanation of the 'how' and 'why' of spontaneous Spirit sightings please see my previous book, **'Voices'**.

During a reading I became aware of a dog that had been in the Spirit World for quite a long time, maybe twenty years or more.

"He's small, with short black fur, and he's overweight! That's the best description I can manage I'm afraid," I said.

"That's OK," the woman sitting opposite me said, "I recognise him anyway. He was my dog when I was a child."

"Well, he's here to say hello to you, obviously," I said. "But he also wants to tell you something."

"Oh?" the woman leant forward, listening, wondering what was coming.

"You have a family dog now that you're a bit worried about," I said. "She sits in the middle of the floor in your lounge, staring into mid-air, seemingly at nothing."

The woman nodded, "That's right," she said. "It's really odd. It's as if she goes into a world of her own, and you've really got to raise your voice to get her attention. I was wondering if I should take her to the Vet's. Maybe she's not well."

"Apparently she's fine," I said, smiling. "She's just watching your dog in the Spirit World. She can see him, you see. So that's what she's staring at," I said. "She isn't ill at all."

A couple of bright, young, chatty girls came for readings. As soon as Kay, the first one to have a reading, sat down opposite me on the sofa in my room, someone in the Spirit World actually threw two British passports onto the table in front of me.

I smiled, "Looks like you're off on your holidays!" I said.

"Yes!" she said. "We've just booked it. We're going next week." She was so thrilled, so excited about it.

But a man's hand suddenly appeared, hovering over the table. Then it descended heavily onto the passports. It was a large hand, and the passports completely disappeared under it.

"Oh dear. I'm sorry to be the bringer of bad news," I said, "but there will be a delay, I'm afraid. You'll have to wait a couple of weeks before you go away. I don't know why. But you *will* go, eventually."

Kay was crestfallen, and it was obvious that she didn't want to believe what I'd said. I couldn't blame her for that!

But three or four days later there was a terrorist attack on a resort near where the girls had booked their holiday. They very quickly transferred their reservation to another country, and went off on holiday three weeks later.

In the middle of a reading with a lady I had never met before, I suddenly saw a 'picture' of a man standing in the middle of a forest. It was a massive forest, and seemed maybe to be located somewhere like Canada. It was certainly not in the UK. He was standing next to a huge tree, smiling into the camera, and holding an axe.

35

"I'm assuming you know someone who used to chop down trees, and who probably travelled abroad with his work," I said.

"Yes," the lady said, "My father was a wood cutter. He travelled abroad a lot. I remember when I was a child he spent quite a bit of time working in the forests of Canada."

My adorable, fun loving Old English Sheepdog, Harry, was a bit of a handful really. His favourite trick was to steal something, maybe a small cushion off a chair, or a tea towel from the kitchen, or something off the vegetable rack – whatever he could reach. Then he would race round the house looking for someone to show his ill-gotten gains to. This was a dog with a sense of humour!

But if anyone was in the back room downstairs, and the door was closed, he would simply throw himself against it, and the force of his weight (he was a big dog) would burst the door open and he would rush into the room, frightening whoever was sitting in there, which on many occasions was my friend Carolyn.

Although Harry's habit of crashing into the room and racing round showing off whatever he had pinched, maybe throwing an apple or a potato in the air, or shaking a cushion about, was very funny, it *was* truly alarming, and not something you would easily forget if you had experienced it. But try as we might it was impossible to stop him doing it.

Harry's eventual loss was a huge blow to me. I missed him terribly.

One day, not many months after he had died, Carolyn and I were sitting in the back room together having a cup of coffee.

It was a bright, calm, sunshiny autumn day, and the empty house was very quiet and peaceful around us. We were engrossed in conversation about some new undertaking Carolyn was just about to start work on, when suddenly, with absolutely no warning, the door burst open and a gust of wind blew sharply across the room.

Although it gave us both a dreadful shock, it also brought us comfort, because we knew immediately that the culprit was Harry. It just had to be. He hadn't lost his wicked sense of humour!

"Your Mum says she went with you last week," I said to the young woman who had come for a reading. "You must have gone away for a day or two for a particular reason."

"Yes," she said, "I went on a training course."

"Well," I said, laughing, "this is what your Mum's saying about it, 'She went to Leamington Spa! Of *all* places, she went to Leamington Spa!'"

And we both laughed.

"She's right!" the young woman said, "I did! My training course was in Leamington Spa!"

"And now your Mum's saying that you're stuck with the boring name 'Smith'," I said. "That's not your name is it?"

"No," the young woman said smiling. "But it *will* be next week, when I get married to my fiancé Steve Smith!"

Chapter Four

The Past

Looking back on our lives and trying to make sense of what we see there is, I think, an integral part of the human condition.

Happy is he who looks only to the future, and never feels the weight of past events tapping him on the shoulder, never feels his gaze pulled unwillingly round to focus on the dark tunnel of his past.

And happy is the individual who has come to terms with that past, for it will not therefore follow him into the future, snapping at his heels; nor will it drag unwelcome, potentially disruptive emotions into his present.

But most of us *need* to revisit our past. We need to try to understand how and why certain situations that remain etched in our memories or on the edges of our consciousness have evolved. We need to trace the fallout from those situations, grasp it, and understand it, as it rumbles on through time, maybe even encroaching on our present day.

That is a crucial part of moving on, of accepting, of understanding, and most of all of finding peace in our lives.

Looking back, my first marriage, to Medium Billy Roberts, was incomprehensible in that it lasted as long as it did.

I have been asked many times over the years to write something about that period in my life, to explain something of what went on in it, in particular what went wrong, and why we were eventually divorced.

I have always resisted the sometimes pressing urge to 'tell all', and to write an expose of that sorry era. I do not intend to do that here, but I *do* intend to try to put the record straight on a number of disconcerting circumstances and events, specifically those whose spectres have followed me into my present, and which still knock on my door today.

I feel sure anyway that the full, unadulterated story of life with my first husband would read like a boring, particularly poorly written, over-exaggerated novel, rather than a factual account of nine years spent in an almost impossible marriage.

So what follows, though deliberately brief, should provide a reasonably clear picture of that era, and go some way towards answering those oft asked questions about that phase in my life, and its repercussions which still breathe down my neck today.

But I must point out that I include this material here only because it is pertinent to the content of this book, and to several particularly memorable events in my life which are outlined in it, and which would not be fully comprehensible without further clarification. In fact, I could not include these events here at all without at least some explanation of the wider picture into which they fit.

As will be obvious, much has been left unsaid, but the lines, as they say, can be read between.

My ex-husband, Billy Roberts, has now been married six times. He has always had a difficult, destructively jealous character, which alone would probably sound the death knell to any relationship, but even worse than that, at least for those who have tried to live with him, is the fact that he has always suffered from an inability to stay away from the opposite sex.

This, combined with his unshakable conviction that absolutely everyone thinks in the same way, along the same lines as *he* does, both male and female, and is therefore constantly plotting to form liaisons with the opposite sex, has created a string of relationships ruined by cheating, lying, mistrust, and to most peoples' ears totally incomprehensible and astounding, but frequently repeated assertions such as:

"Don't tell anyone you used to live in Paris or they'll all know that you're a slag."

My astonished reply on hearing this bizarre command directed at me for the first of many times was, "Why on earth would anyone think *that*?"

"Because only a slag would live for so long in Paris," he said.

The problem here, as with all his many outlandish assertions, was that he really did believe them. There was no reasoning with him.

"He's only joking," I told the volunteer in the coffee shop at the local Spiritualist Church where Billy, as the visiting Medium, was taking the service that day. She had heard what he said to me, and was staring in amazement at Billy's back as he walked off. She shook her head, looked over at me, said nothing, and continued washing cups.

But it was his womanising that really hurt, although I was not aware at the time just how extensive that was. Looking back with the benefit of hindsight, I realise now that I missed all the tell-tale signs, and misinterpreted all the hints dropped in my direction by well-meaning acquaintances. I was living in a dream world, and of course the flimsy walls of that world eventually came tumbling down around me.

So why didn't I leave him long before I actually did? Well, the short answer is that I had, at that time, nowhere to run to. Returning to Folkestone, where I had lived previously, seemed my best bet, and that *was* eventually where I went.

But of course it was actually considerably more complicated than that. I suppose I was just one of those women who had unwittingly dug themselves a deep, miserable, relationship-hole in life, and fallen into it. It took me several years to pull myself out and find somewhere to go, somewhere to start my life over again, and the courage with which to do so.

Although throughout the years we were constantly short of money, Billy would not allow me to go out to work anywhere without him because, in his opinion,

"Women only go out to work to find another man."

Unfortunately, the county bailiffs had little or no sympathy with that opinion, and so one rainy autumn day I said goodbye to the television and the small amount of furniture that had graced the front room.

Always on the lookout for money from any easy source, he made £50 from the sale of my beautiful, much loved watch, which had been a gift from my mother, and then screamed at me when I cried.

The erroneous conviction that I was continually searching around for another man was at the forefront of his thoughts day and night. He would seldom let me out of his sight, not even trusting me to go food shopping alone. On the rare occasion that I did he would 'smell another man' on me on my return home. I grew weary of the constant shouting, the constant groundless, ridiculous accusations, and the constant refrain of, "I'll never trust you!"

Billy would continually accuse me of looking at men reflected through the wing mirror of the car as we were driving, or of staring at men walking by on the pavement, or of deliberately *avoiding* staring at a man, in order to hide the fact that I actually *wanted* to stare. I could not win.

My ex- husband's existence was, and probably still is, ruled by the corrosive influence of his uncontrollable jealousy, reaching into and tainting or destroying every aspect of his life, and the lives of those around him. I spent a great deal of time, energy and tears, trying desperately to find a way to counter, to dissipate that constant stream of negativity. But it was impossible, and I eventually gave up.

It was only some considerable time after I had finally left him that the full picture emerged, and I discovered just how far his duplicitous scheming and plotting had reached where *I* was concerned. Over the years a great many people have been only too happy to seek me out in order to enlighten me, to join up the dots and fill in the picture. Most of these people have their own stories to tell where my ex-husband is concerned, and are only too willing to do so.

However, his wide ranging knowledge of the Paranormal, and his occasionally charismatic work as a Medium, at one time made him something of an attractive proposition to the opposite sex, and therefore allowed him to grasp the opportunities he craved in life. He found himself, by virtue of the gift of mediumship, in something of a position of power, surrounded for the most part by vulnerable people, often at exceedingly difficult times in their lives.

I remember being devastated, and so ashamed, when a group of women, regular visitors to the Psychic Centre we ran at one time, drew me aside one evening and told me they would not be coming there again. It seemed that my husband had by that time propositioned each one of them. They were not impressed. They hugged me as they left.

That incident marked the beginning of the end of the marriage.

After so many years have passed I still see one or two of those women occasionally. Although they always ask what work I'm doing, and if I'm still involved in the world of the Paranormal, they have never once mentioned my ex-husband, or what happened at the Psychic Centre. But I can still feel their pity for me, the cuckolded wife who, incredibly, wasn't aware of her husband's transgressions.

Always the consummate actor, the real nature of the man remained for the most part hidden from the public, at least during the years of our marriage, and I must bear most of the blame for that, as my silence on oh so many situations served only to protect him.

But those few of my friends with whom I managed, with considerable difficulty, to retain contact, began to think I had lost my mind, and that I would never succeed in regaining my freedom.

My father was an alcoholic, though a functioning one, for the greater part of his life. This very fact was incredibly useful to Billy Roberts, and unbeknown to me he used it against me, for his own ends, time and time again.

In those early years we travelled a great deal around the north of England, regularly meeting new people at Spiritualist Churches and workshops.

He would 'set the scene' so to speak, often saying, "My wife is an alcoholic," as almost an opening remark when meeting someone new. He would usually follow that with, "Her father has been an alcoholic all his life."

However, simply describing me as an alcoholic would very probably not have achieved the desired effect, for few people would, I suspect, instantly react with hostility towards someone unfortunate enough to suffer from an alcohol dependency problem. It was, though, a step in the right direction, which Billy then followed up, time and time again, with a myriad of other outlandish, negative claims about me.

Over the years I have probably heard them all, from a number of different sources, including two of his other ex-wives.

But the obvious question is, why oh why did he do it? And here I just don't have the answer. He was simply marching to the beat of his own drum, seeking to create the impression that he was married to some kind of monster, in order to achieve his own ends, whatever *they* may have been.

One of the most cruel and hurtful situations you can ever find yourself in is to discover that someone, a complete stranger to you, someone you have never even spoken to, really does not like you, but you have absolutely no idea *why*.

I now know that my ex-husband deliberately placed me in this type of situation on many occasions, to achieve his own dubious ends. A number of these scenarios really stand out, and remain crystal clear in my memory to this day. So does the awful hurt I felt as a consequence.

"Death is for many of us the gate of hell; but we are inside on the way out, not outside on the way in."
George Bernard Shaw

Chapter Five

The Stage Door

Hiring a theatre and producing an 'Evening of Clairvoyance' there, with all the associated costs of advertising, promotion, sound and lighting set up was, and probably still is, expensive. Although 'stage mediumship' was all Billy wanted to do at that time, we could not afford to do it very often. Money was always tight.

So when the President of a large and well established Spiritualist Church in the south of England offered to fund a tour of UK theatres for Billy, albeit alongside another Medium, Billy jumped at the chance.

I had met the Church President only once previously, simply to say hello to, on the single occasion that Billy did an 'Evening of Clairvoyance' at his Church on the south coast. But I knew little or nothing about him.

All the arrangements for the forthcoming tour were sorted out over the phone between Billy and Mr P, as I will call him. I was not involved in any way. I did not need to be.

But one day, shortly before the tour was due to begin, I received a very strange phone call from Mr P in which he told me not to bother accompanying Billy to the first theatre on the tour.

"He doesn't need you there; there's absolutely no reason for you to come; I've got everything sorted out," he told me. "The theatre's not far from where you live so Billy can find it himself. And we're not staying overnight, so he can drive there and back in the same evening."

45

I was stunned, bemused, and hardly knew how to reply.

"Umm, I usually go to all the events with Billy," I said lamely, wondering why this man, who I barely knew, did not want me at the theatre. After all, I was not involved in the organisation of the event, and would simply be just another member of the audience, watching the show, but playing no part in any of it.

"Well, you don't need to go to *this* one," he said, his voice rising slightly in both volume and pitch. There was now an unmistakable note of aggression in what he said, somehow accentuating the already clearly discernible southern twang in his voice.

"Umm, well.... I'll ask Billy," I said, not really knowing what else to say at that point.

"Don't bother asking him!" he said. "Just don't turn up there." And he put the phone down none too gently. I heard the clatter as it hit the base unit before the line went dead.

I stared at the receiver in my hand, wondering what on earth this man's problem was. Why didn't he want me to go to the theatre? What possible difference would it make if I was there?

As I replaced the phone a little voice in my head told me that it would be nice to have an evening off, an evening alone, to relax and be able to do what I wanted for a change. I could do a bit of reading, and maybe some writing. And I thought it would probably be very agreeable not to have to spend time with such a rude, aggressive man.

But I just *knew* that was not going to happen. I knew it because Billy never went anywhere alone. *Never.*

And sure enough, when I told him what had happened he wouldn't even discuss that strange phone call, and certainly wouldn't hear of me staying at home while he drove to the theatre alone.

"But he doesn't want me to go," I said, "He made that *very* clear. He was incredibly rude to me. Have you any idea *why?* It's not as if I even *know* the man."

"No, no idea," Billy said, "but you're going."

"Look, for some reason he really doesn't want me there, so it'll probably cause a huge amount of bad feeling if I *do* go," I said, "and do you know what, I'd really rather *not* go."

"You're going," Billy repeated.

And that was that. There was no point arguing.

But I wondered about Mr P's attitude towards me. At that point I was curious about it, rather than upset, but I began to worry about the forthcoming tour. Nine theatres meant a lot of turning up where I wasn't wanted.

I could see a dark cloud of potential problems gathering on the horizon.

Having arrived early in the evening at the first theatre on the tour, which wasn't far from home, Billy and I sat in one of the small, basic dressing rooms, waiting. I tried to read while Billy readied himself for the show.

But I found it hard to concentrate. I was anxious, worried about what Mr P would say when he saw me; what his attitude would be towards me when he realised I had not heeded his 'advice' to stay away. And because I didn't know what his problem with me was, it would be difficult to know how to react.

Eventually, about an hour before the show was due to start there was a knock at the dressing room door, it opened, and Mr P came in.

He seemed rather shorter than I remembered, and the long, heavy, dark brown mackintosh he wore looked somehow odd on him, giving him the appearance of an ageing, over weight, failed actor, still desperately playing a role. His face was red, as if he had been running against the wind, his eyes were bloodshot, and it looked as if he hadn't shaved that day. He was probably only about the age of sixty, although he appeared to be considerably older.

He and Billy shook hands and exchanged greetings, and then Mr P introduced his companion, who had followed him into the room. This was Andy, the second Medium, who would be working on stage with Billy.

Having completely ignored me until then, not even glancing in my direction, or acknowledging my presence in any way, Mr P suddenly turned to me and said, "So, you just couldn't stay away then?" in a voice brimming with contempt. The unpleasant, mocking grin on his face matched his tone of voice. I heard his friend snigger. The decidedly awkward situation obviously amused him.

As Mr P had begun to speak to me I suddenly became aware of his aura flowing around him. Its colours and shades of dark, muddy brown, flecked with points of bright red light here and there, washed over his body, and over his face. I had seldom seen such clearly defined auric colours, and this spontaneous manifestation stunned me. Such a thing rarely happened to me, and I stared at him, fascinated. I could feel wave after wave of his anger directed towards me. It was so strong I could almost reach out and touch it, as if it were somehow a living thing.

I opened my mouth to respond, to tell him exactly *why* I was there, but I instantly thought better of it, and instead, although it took something of an effort, I remained silent. No one wanted any friction or arguments just before presenting a live show. That would certainly not have been fair, either to performers or audience.

The moment passed, Mr P turned away, gestured to Billy to accompany him, and then the three men left the room to go and check on the sound and lighting arrangements for the show. The door slammed shut behind them.

Left alone I felt shaky, tearful, miserable, but most of all I felt mystified. What could possibly be the reason for Mr P's attitude towards me?

Eventually I went and found a seat in the audience, on the back row, far from the stage, where I remained until the show finished later that evening.

Driving home afterwards I said, "Look, this is *so* awkward. He obviously doesn't like me. Has he told you *why*? I don't even *know* the man, so what could I have done to make him dislike me so much?"

"I've no idea," Billy said. "Maybe he just doesn't like women."

"Well I can't go to the next venue," I said. "He was bad enough with me *this* time. Just imagine what he'll be like at the next one if I turn up again."

"You're coming!" Billy said. "I'm not going on my own."

In fact, going to the theatres on the tour, and facing the nasty, sarcastic comments aimed at me by Mr P was in fact the lesser of two evils. There would be an end to it eventually, when the tour was over. It was therefore preferable to *not* going, and thereby having to endure hours of shouting from my irate husband.

So the tour continued, and I was a reluctant observer at each show. I was trapped, caught in a situation I didn't understand, with no obvious exit strategy.

At one theatre, maybe the fourth or fifth in the tour, Mr P came into the dressing room just before the start of the show carrying a tray of drinks.

"Dutch courage!" he said, putting the tray down on the ubiquitous small, wooden table in the middle of the room, and passing Billy a glass of wine.

"And it shouldn't take *you* a minute to polish this lot off," he said, sniggering and pushing the tray across the table towards me. There were four full glasses of wine on it.

I stared blankly at the tray, wondering what on earth this unpleasant man was doing. What was he playing at?

"You've wasted your money," I told him as I picked my book up and left the room, heading for the auditorium and a seat in the audience for the rest of the evening.

"What did he do that for?" I asked Billy later, on the way home. "He usually brings *you* a drink and just ignores me. He's never given me a drink before, and now he gives me *four* glasses. What's going on? Why did he do that?"

"No idea," Billy said.

"Well, I'm going to ask him, *and* I'm going to ask him why he dislikes me so much, and what I've done to make him behave so badly towards me all the time," I said.

"No you are *not!*" Billy almost shouted, "You're *not* going to say a word to him. He might get annoyed and pull out of the tour, and it'll be *your* fault." He glared at me. I sighed.

And so I did not confront Mr P, but instead kept away from him as much as possible. I simply tried to ignore his nastiness, not wishing to cause an argument just before a live show, or risk the curtailment of the tour. But his behaviour towards me grew worse and worse, and would have been unacceptable under *any* circumstances, even if I *had* done something to warrant it.

By the time we reached the seventh of nine theatre venues, three weeks later, I rarely waited in the dressing room with Billy before a show, but usually found myself a seat in the auditorium early on, and read a book until the show began. The less I saw of Mr P the better.

But I was upset. It was a ridiculous, hurtful and incomprehensible situation to be in, and I couldn't wait for the tour to end.

That day finally dawned with the last show at a theatre in Yorkshire.

The drive across country to the venue, though long, was very pleasant. The early autumn sun shone, and it was unseasonably warm, though heavy rain was forecast later. I tried to be positive, and kept telling myself that it would soon all be over, and I would probably never have to endure Mr P's company again. I held on to that happy, comforting thought.

The theatre had been built in Victorian days and it was small and attractive, with the original wooden frontage painted cream and green, and still in good repair. It wasn't far from the town centre and we found it easily. Having parked the car opposite the theatre we walked across the road to the front doors. They were locked and there was no one about. It was only four o'clock, so we walked round the back, into a small square, and up to the stage door, arriving there just as a group of schoolchildren and their teacher were pouring out of it, laughing and talking excitedly. It seemed they had been rehearsing a play all day, and the thespian life suited them. They had loved it.

The teacher held the stage door open for us. We thanked her and went inside.

The door was made of metal. It was actually a heavy security door, and it closed and locked automatically by means of a horizontal metal bar on the inside, half way down. It could only be opened from the inside by pressing downwards on the bar, and pushing hard. It could not be opened from the outside at all.

The sound of the door clanging shut behind us now only emphasised the fact that it was very quiet inside the theatre, almost eerily quiet. The corridor we found ourselves in was narrow and dimly lit, stretching out in front of us like the entrance to a burrow, with no visible sign of any doors off it.

There was an odd, musty smell in the air that spoke of old wooden floorboards and years of accumulated dust. The atmosphere seemed to press heavily down on us, as if we had suddenly, unaccountably found ourselves in a cavern, hundreds of feet below ground. It felt as though we were walking through a thick cloud of discarded emotions, of passions and excitements generated and amassed over the years, and which now reached out for our attention, desperate to make their presence felt.

We walked slowly down the corridor in search of a dressing room. I had to resist the temptation to tip toe across the bare floorboards as quietly as I could, to avoid disturbing the peaceful, whispering silence of the old building, which seemed to live and breathe around us.

At the end of the corridor we found a door with 'Dressing Room A' written on a small piece of paper and pinned to it. We opened the door, went in and put the light on.

We found exactly what you would expect to find in a small theatre dressing room – a round, wooden table, which had certainly seen better days, in the middle of the room, with three old and unsteady wooden chairs round it. There was a mirror on the wall, next to a small, grimy window covered with metal netting, and affording a view of a brick wall outside. An old, somewhat warped sliding door opened onto a tiny bathroom.

I sat down on one of the chairs, thinking how glad I was that this was the last show on the tour. I had had enough.

Shortly after, the calm stillness in the theatre was shattered by the sound of loud talking in the corridor outside Dressing Room A. It heralded the arrival of Mr P and his friend Andy, the other Medium.

Billy opened the door and greeted them. They were laughing,

"We only got into the theatre because the manager was leaving just as we arrived," Mr P said, "All the doors are locked and there's no one else here. We thought we might have to break in through a window! The manager has had to go out, but he says he'll be back in time to open up to the public at 7pm. Until then we're on our own."

He was standing in the corridor next to a door with 'Dressing Room B' scrawled on it in white paint, and now he reached out and opened it, "Come on in," he said to Billy.

The three men disappeared into the room and closed the door behind them. I could hear them laughing and talking loudly. I stood up and shut the door, then settled down to read until the show started.

I soon became engrossed in what I was reading, and was startled some time later when the door was suddenly thrown open, and Mr P strode into the room.

"As you've turned up again you may as well earn your keep," he said in his usual unpleasant, aggressive tone. "Billy wants a bottle of water to put on the stage with him when he's working. You can get one from that shop round the corner on the main street." And he turned to leave the room.

"Err; hang on a moment," I said, "No. I'll go later when the manager is in the theatre. Otherwise I won't be able to get back in again."

Mr P stopped, one hand on the door handle, and stared at me over his shoulder. I stared back at the cold and hostile expression on his lined, unshaven face.

"OK", he said, "I'll wait at the stage door and let you back in."

The same dull brown colours and nuances that I had seen before showed suddenly around him in his aura, flecked with bright red. I knew he was lying.

"I'll go later," I repeated.

He suddenly turned and shouted across the corridor; "Billy!" and Billy appeared in the doorway. "You want the water now, don't you?" Mr P asked.

"Yep. Get me two bottles will you?" Billy said in my direction.

"Who's going to let me back in?" I asked, looking straight at Billy. He looked away, unwilling to meet my eyes.

"I've already *told* you; *I'll* wait at the door," Mr P said testily, shaking his head, feigning exasperation.

So, reluctantly I picked up my bag and walked past the two of them, out of the dressing room and along the corridor. I stopped at the heavy stage door and looked back. In the dim light I could see that all three men were standing outside the dressing rooms watching me.

"I won't be long. Maybe five minutes," I called.

Mr P began walking towards me, "Go on," he said, "I'll wait at the door."

I leant on the bar, pushed, and the heavy door grated open. I stepped outside. The door swung creakily back, and clanged shut behind me. There was a moment of complete silence.

Daylight was beginning to fade, and a gentle rain had started to fall. There was now a chill mist in the air that reminded me suddenly of time spent in the Scottish hills as a child. I quickly pushed away the sad, maudlin feeling that the memory brought with it, and which threatened to overwhelm me. I couldn't afford the luxury of sentiment at that particular moment in my life.

I walked quickly across the small square and along the pavement towards the corner, shivering, and wishing I had thought to bring my coat with me. There was no one about, but I could hear the sound of a car or two on the main road ahead. I rounded the corner and saw the shop a couple of blocks down. Its lights stood out, shimmering through the gathering gloom.

Having bought two bottles of water I walked quickly back the way I had come, round the corner and along the road towards the back of the theatre. The rain became increasingly heavy, and by the time I reached the stage door it was hammering down and I was soaked.

I knocked on the door. The heavy metal seemed to absorb the sound, and I knocked again, harder. But I knew. I just knew.

I knew that no one was waiting inside to open the door and let me in. Not Mr P, not Billy. No one.

I tried again, anger lending strength to my arm, and force to my knuckles. But of course the door remained closed. Had I really expected it to open?

I turned away and stood with my back to it, as the hot tears prickled my eyes and spilled down my face. The pent up emotions that had been gnawing away at me over the past couple of months threatened to spill out and overwhelm me. I felt angry and I felt sorry for myself. Doubtless I had been stupid to want to believe that I would be able to get back in to the theatre, that they would open the door for me.

But most of all I felt miserable, because I didn't know what I had done to deserve all this. I didn't know why I was being treated like a pariah.

The rain continued to fall; the drops bouncing off the paving stones in the square, leaving them bright and glistening as they reflected the pale orange light shed by half a dozen nearby street lamps.

My hair dripped small, icy cold drops of moisture onto my face to mingle with the tears there, and my pullover had begun to feel uncomfortably damp and cold against my back. I shivered again.

I nearly missed the unfamiliar sound as I fished in my pocket for a tissue. But I suddenly realised what it was as I pushed the wet hair back off my face, and dabbed at my eyes. I whipped round in time to see the stage door swinging slowly open, its old, rusty hinges creaking and groaning as it went.

Gratefully I sprang at it, grabbed it, and lunged inside the theatre out of the increasingly cold and wet evening.

"Oh thank you! Thank you!" I said breathlessly, again pushing my cold, damp hair off my face and out of my eyes, and looking round through the gloom to see who had opened the door, who had rescued me.

But there was no one there. The corridor was empty. I stared down it towards the dressing rooms. Nothing moved there amongst the encroaching shadows. There was no sign of Mr P or Billy.

The grating clang behind me made me jump. The door had closed and the bar had ratcheted into place. I turned to look at it. How had it opened, I wondered?

Who had opened it? And where were they now?

I stood perfectly still in the silence of the old theatre, waiting for something to happen, trying to read the atmosphere.

And then I saw him. He was standing in the shadows at the end of the corridor, almost hidden there behind the door.

The gentle golden glow around the upper part of his body told me that this was a Spirit entity, a visitor from the Spirit World. I stared, enthralled, knowing without a doubt that he had come to see *me*, because although it had been many years since the first and only other time I had seen this man, I recognised him immediately.

He was wearing the same simple dark uniform, with a high collar, and gold buttons, that I had seen him wearing before. The shiny peak of his black cap shadowed his eyes, but I knew that there would be a ghost of a smile on his kind and gentle face. There just had to be.

This was the man who had appeared to me at a time of great unhappiness in my childhood, and whose single word, "Courage," uttered then, has stayed with me, and brought me comfort, throughout my life. (See 'Ghost of a Smile').

At that moment, in the theatre, I still did not know who he was. It would be several more years before I found that out.

And then he was gone. He had vanished back into the Spirit World having been visible to me in that gloomy corridor for no more than ten seconds.

But that was enough. It was enough time to recognise him and feel the strength of his compassion.

I was so very grateful to him. I felt elated, and as always, I felt privileged to be so clearly reminded that the Spirit

World is just a thought away, and is watching the unhappy turmoil in our lives.

Even the briefest of visitations from the Spirit World brings with it a feeling of euphoria. It has always been so in my life, and this occasion was no different.

I walked as if on air slowly back down the corridor and stopped outside the dressing rooms at the end. I needed a couple of minutes to compose myself and replace the smile on my face with a more suitable, neutral expression. I could hear Billy and Mr P talking inside; they were talking about me. They found it amusing that it was raining so heavily, and that I would probably be soaked by now, as I waited in vain outside the stage door.

I opened the dressing room door and walked in. The laughter stopped abruptly as all three men turned and stared at me. There was complete silence as they waited to see what I would say, what I would do. But without looking at any of them I simply reached out and put the two bottles of water on the table, turned and left the room without uttering a word. I closed the door quietly behind me.

Mr P's shocked expression, caught from the corner of my eye, was almost comical. I was glad.

I made my way to the auditorium and found a seat there. I felt elated as I replayed that brief Spirit visitation again and again in my memory. Mr P and his appalling treatment of me could not have mattered less at that moment, or at any moment since. I would never have to see him again. In that instant, as I had gazed at my Spirit visitor, I had been reminded that other things were so much more important, and life fell back into context once again.

I was lucky, so very lucky. I have always known that.

I never did see Mr P again, and no one in that dressing room on that memorable day ever asked me how I had managed to get back into the theatre. But of course, no one ever apologised for failing to wait at the stage door, and to open it for me.

Chapter Six
Citizens Band Radio

Even when staggering blindly around in the dark depths of despair, we humans may often find a reason to smile, to giggle, or even to roar with laughter. That is the nature of the resilient human psyche.

One evening, some time after the events of the 'stage door', I was working at my desk in the living room at home.

It was very quiet. The house was empty. Billy was out. He had told me he was going for a drive, but as it was ten o'clock at night I rather doubted that. However, I didn't care anymore where he went or what he did, and I never questioned him. Having dithered and vacillated for so long, I had finally had enough of a difficult and loveless marriage. I was beginning to realise that the decision to leave, and start my life again somewhere else, was staring me in the face, and looking more and more inviting with every passing day.

The phone rang. It seemed rather late for a phone call, but I answered it and heard a voice say, "Err.... Err.... I'm sorry, but is that Mrs Roberts?"

It was the voice of a well-spoken, elderly man, and I was pretty sure that I didn't know him. He spoke slowly, carefully, enunciating each word, as if he may once have been a school teacher or lecturer.

"Yes, it is," I said.

"Ah, yes...." he said, and paused. I waited, wondering what he wanted, and why he was phoning at that time.

"Are you….are you…. quite…. *well*?" he asked.

How very odd, I thought. I hoped this wasn't going to be a 'strange' phone call. "Yes, thank you," I said, "I'm fine; very well. How can I help you?"

There was another, longer pause, and then, "Well", the gentleman said, "I suppose I had better just come right out…. and, err, tell you. That seems probably the best thing to do in the circumstances."

I waited, wondering what on earth was coming.

"Are you married to someone called 'Billy Roberts'?" he asked, his voice trembling slightly.

"Yes, I am," I said.

"Well, you're the right person then," he said.

"Am I?" I said, feeling like giggling.

"Yes…. My wife and I have been trying to reach a decision for three months. We just couldn't decide whether to tell you or not. But we've finally decided that we really have to," he said.

"You have to what?" I asked him, curious now.

"Err….We have to tell you that your husband is having an affair," the gentleman said. "Do you know that?"

"Umm…. Well….actually yes, yes I do," I said. "But how do *you* know?"

I was completely taken aback, stunned that a total stranger would ring me out of the blue to tell me that my husband was having an affair. Why on earth would this man do that, I wondered, why would he get involved? He didn't know me from Adam. And anyway, how did *he* know what Billy was getting up to?

"Ah, well…." He said, "You see, my wife and I have a Citizens Band Radio. We listen to it most evenings, and pick up all sorts of fascinating transmissions. It's a very interesting pastime. We're in a CB club, you see. But over the last three or four months we have heard your husband regularly speaking to someone called 'Sue', and it became obvious that she wasn't his wife.

59

You see, your husband *always* says that *you* are drunk. We heard him just ten minutes ago. He was telling Sue that you were lying on the living room floor, almost unconscious, having drunk two bottles of wine. So, **this** time I said to my wife, 'That's it! That's enough! Let's find out if that's true.'

So we rang you. And it obviously **isn't** true.... unless of course you're speaking to me from the floor!"

"Oh....that is *soo* funny!" I said, trying not to laugh, but giggling anyway. "I *have* frequently heard that he tells lots of people I'm an alcoholic."

"Well, yes," the gentleman said. "But he has been telling Sue a lot worse than that about you too! Actually, some of the things he has said are quite appalling."

"Don't worry, I've probably heard most of them," I told him.

"Well, we didn't like what we heard," the gentleman said, "and we didn't believe it either. That's why we decided to try to find out; to see if we could speak to you."

"Well, thank you," I said, "I'm really glad that you did."

"I'll send you a tape of your husband speaking to his lady friend," the gentleman said, "We've got one or two. You may find it very interesting!"

Sure enough, true to his word, a tape arrived in the post shortly after this conversation. I have it to this day.

Chapter Seven
The Curse

Not so long ago, following a series of futile attempts to disrupt my life in a number of different ways, a misguided and, as it turned out, seriously misinformed woman put what she considered to be a curse on me.

She had bombarded me for some months with letters, phone calls and text messages, one of which came at three in the morning from a mobile phone belonging to someone who I knew to be dead.

Having got no response from me to any of this, she had obviously decided to enlist what she thought would be a helping hand from the supernatural – a curse.

The dirty, dog eared envelope arrived in the post. Unsuspecting, I opened it. It contained a deliberately distorted, black and white photo of a nondescript woman, which had a tuft of coarse hair roughly taped to the bottom of it.

I assume the hair was supposed to have come from a human head, but it actually looked very much as if it had come from some kind of elderly animal. It was dirty, scruffy, and unpleasant.

I do not know if the photo was supposed to be a likeness of me, or of the woman who had sent it to me. It was impossible to tell.

I had never met her, and never seen her, but I did know who she was, and over the years I had learned something of her strange, rather twisted character and odd, blinkered, self-centred and greedy outlook on life. She was a bully.

An accompanying grubby page, torn from a notebook of some kind, contained at the top a series of unintelligible squiggles, underneath which was a threat to curse me eternally, and from beyond the grave.

This 'curse' and the manner in which I received it, is in fact dangerous.

But not to me.

The 'curse' is dangerous **to the woman who sent it to me,** and who evidently has no knowledge or understanding of the workings of 'thought dynamics'.

The very act of deliberately wishing someone ill, or of sending out evil, injurious thoughts towards another person, is an act which carries within it the dangerous possibility of *retribution*; that is, of your own evil thoughts *returning* and descending upon *you* ten times stronger than when you sent them out.

Maybe you have never considered the possibility that your thoughts are living things? Well, indeed they are!

Just as light, heat and odour may be considered as 'things', so too may our thoughts be considered to be 'things' i.e. *living* things; the strongest of which may actually be seen and felt by a Medium or psychic.

In the course of our everyday lives a quick, simple, albeit selfish remark such as "I really don't like that person! I hope she doesn't get the job. She doesn't deserve it!" does not carry much strength within it, because you yourself have not infused it with much energy. You have not spent a great deal of time preparing it, you have not concentrated on it, and maybe you do not actually mean what you say. In fact you probably do not care at all, one way or another, about that person's employment prospects, and this was simply a throwaway remark motivated only by low level jealousy.

In this example it hardly matters whether the person you are talking about deserves, or does not deserve to get the job.

Nonetheless, your thought, once released from your control, will travel to the object of your dislike rather like a small, dark arrow, and land on that person's aura. But, having little or no energy, it will bounce harmlessly off again, unable to penetrate their protective shell.

Your thought will not return to you in this instance, and will simply dissolve back into nothingness, devoid of the little energy it once had.

However, spend a considerable amount of time concentrating on how much you really hate someone, and focusing on how much you wish them ill; maybe visualise them failing disastrously in their life, or falling seriously ill; imagine them struggling through their days facing problem after problem and never finding happiness....

These thoughts will leave you as if they were veritable missiles. For you have truly energised and vitalised them with Prana*, and sent them off as living things to do your bidding.

They will land in a vicious, determined hail on the unfortunate person's aura, ready to wreak havoc on that person's life.

*Prana is 'universal energy', which is found in all things, both animate and inanimate. A strong thought of any kind, either negative or positive, attracts universal energy to itself, and is coloured and vitalised by the amount of Prana it holds. The stronger the thought, the greater the amount of Prana it holds, and it is in fact that Prana which is responsible for turning our thoughts into living things.

But let's pause a moment here to consider the notion of Universal Justice, of Fate, of Karma, and of the part they play in this scenario, i.e. in this scenario of 'thought dynamics'.

If the person you wish to harm, to damage and injure, even to destroy, does *not* deserve your wrath, let alone your malicious attack upon them, how is it then just or fair that they should suffer in any way because of you?

The answer is that if they are undeserving of your attack, your 'thought missiles' will be unable to penetrate the protection of the aura around that person, and will therefore rebound harmlessly from them, *and return to you*, gaining energy as they go.

Your jealous, cruel and vindictive thoughts will return speedily from whence they came, and crash into your aura upon their return, ten times stronger than when they began their journey.

And should you continue over time sending out unjustified thought attacks, thereby causing your aura to be bombarded by the returning evil thoughts, *your* evil thoughts, you will in due course reap the inevitable consequences. You will be punished *by* such things and not *for* them, i.e. you will suffer the consequences you intended to impose on others.

The living thoughts will eventually be numerous enough and strong enough to break completely through the protection of your aura. Your vicious and nasty 'thought missiles' will begin to infiltrate, to burrow in, and to cause you significant harm in your physical existence.

You may become seriously ill; you may encounter insurmountable problems in your life; you will certainly never find happiness. In fact, that which you wished upon an undeserving other or others will descend upon *you*. And why shouldn't it? The working of Universal Law cannot be scorned.

We routinely fill our close psychic environment with living thoughts in the course of our everyday lives, the vast majority of which simply dissolve harmlessly back into the ether.

But the perpetrators of undeserved, harmful criticism, and of offensive, thoughtless comment; and those who unfairly target others for *any* reason, or who bear a grudge against another, allowing it to eat away at their mind over time; or those whose lives are ruled by jealousy towards others, to the exclusion of all else........ *All* create an undesirable, intolerable environment around themselves, as the residue of their offensive thoughts hangs invisibly around them like a cloud of razor sharp barbed wire.

You would not have to be psychic to sense this environment. Most people would be aware of a certain indefinable, unpleasant 'something' around an individual, sensed rather than seen, and would eventually feel uncomfortable, or awkward in its presence. They may henceforth seek to avoid 'it', although they would probably not know why.

The comments, "I'm not keen on Mr A. Not sure why. I just don't really like him," or, "I feel awkward around Mrs B. It's nothing she says, it's just a feeling I get when I'm talking to her," are probably particularly apt here. We have all experienced those seemingly inexplicable, disagreeable feelings.

It is perhaps apposite to mention here that 'like will attract like' in the world of thought dynamics i.e. there is a strong tendency for thought to attract to itself , like a magnet, other thoughts which are similar in character, which will then merge and blend together into 'thought strata' in the astral space, rather like clouds. This collective 'thought environment', created by the people who live together in a community such as a town, a city, a country, or even those who work together in a large corporation, will strongly

65

influence the thoughts of the individuals who spend most of their time there.

This is of course the 'stuff' that *inspiration* is made of. How many times have we heard musicians or songwriters for example tell us that they feel they are sometimes able to 'tap into' a flow of creative ideas, but have no inkling where such a flow comes from. Well, it comes from like-minds, which have at one time worked on and created those ideas, or the music, but have either not finished their work for one reason or another, or maybe not had the ability to put it into marketable form. They have, however, as a result of their hard work, loaded their ideas with Prana, and sent them out into the ether where they may one day be attracted towards the similar thoughts of a like-minded, inspiration seeking individual. That individual may therefore find the mine of creative ideas he is searching for.

As the thoughts sent out by individuals attract and are attracted by thought of a similar nature, there is of course, over time, a self-perpetuating, strengthening effect upon the collective thought environment. Again, one does not have to be psychic to feel its influence. We have all visited areas where we felt distinctly ill at ease, or perhaps lived in a town where we just knew we did not fit in, where we felt we had little in common with the views or lifestyle of the other residents.

On the other hand we can probably all recall feeling 'at home' in a particular region or city, feeling a sense of warm familiarity with it, and knowing that we would be happy to live there.

The corporate culture in any large company is not created hap hazardly by accident, but grows from the accumulated, combined thoughts of those who work there.

Houses and other buildings will also absorb the character of the strongest thoughts, whether good, bad, or evil, of those living or spending time there. Which of us has not, at one time or another, walked into a house and immediately felt so uncomfortable there that we wanted to walk right back out the door, and remove ourselves from that unpleasant environment. We may have experienced a feeling of fear, of terror, or a sense of evil in the vicinity, or maybe simply felt a low level, nagging conviction that we just had to leave that place. This is because the predominant thoughts of the house's former inhabitants still live on there, and will settle like an invisible cloud over any newcomer, whose subsequent experience of this thought environment will vary to a greater or lesser degree, depending on the level of development of their own sensitive nature.

To some people the atmosphere in that house will seem nothing less than intolerable; to others it will be no more than mildly disturbing. But this inhospitable atmosphere *can* be changed. An individual whose life is filled with strong positive and kindly thought will soon be able to overcome the gloomy and depressing thought environment left by any number of previous occupants, and impose his own atmosphere on the house.

And of course we have probably all experienced the exhilarating feeling of entering a house which possesses a bright, positive and happy thought environment, and most of us will consciously strive to create something similar in our own homes.

Finally, it is worth mentioning here that those individuals who routinely fill their personal psychic space with evil thoughts of a wicked and hateful nature, will eventually attract to themselves the environment and circumstances necessary to provide him/her with the opportunity to put those aberrant thoughts into action in some way, to gratify their corrupt desires, whatever they may be.

Conversely, he who cultivates thought of the highest and kindliest nature will move upward through situations of harmony and wellbeing in his life.

The lesson is simple, although putting it into practice in our lives is far from simple. Make space in your mind only for the highest and best of thoughts. Banish, if you can, the mean, jealous, unworthy thoughts, no matter how small and fleeting they may be, and never, ever direct any strong, negative thoughts against another person, for Universal Law dictates that you will surely suffer the grim consequences, one way or another, of your desire to impose harm on an undeserving other.

Those people who deliberately aim unwarranted thought attacks at others should never be arrogant enough to imagine that in doing so there will be no consequences for themselves, or that they will remain untouched, unscathed and anonymous. Your thoughts may be invisible, and may remain hidden and unknown to most, but *they* know their provenance, and given the right circumstances those living thoughts will return and descend upon you in force.

We are each responsible not just for our actions, but for our thoughts too.

You can be sure that your very own chickens *will* return home to roost.

Any reader who is interested in looking further into the concept of 'thought dynamics' might like to have a look at the book: *'Fourteen Lessons in Yogi Philosophy and Oriental Occultism' by Yogi Ramacharaka.*

Chapter Eight

Scraggy

One of the greatest joys in my life is keeping ex battery chickens.

We collect them from wherever the British Hen Welfare Trust has managed to persuade a farmer to release them, rather than send them to the abattoir, and we load them into cardboard boxes, and bring them home.

During the drive they remain totally silent and unmoving, for they are traumatised, petrified, overwhelmed.

These chickens have lived all their lives in cages with numerous others. They have eaten the same food day after day. They have never seen natural daylight, never felt the chill of wind or rain on their feathers, and never felt the warmth of the sun.

They have never had the opportunity to do natural chickeny things, to stroll about through the grass, to scratch for seeds in the soil, to run about and jump onto tree stumps or branches, just for the fun of it, and to enjoy their lives.

So for the first couple of days after they arrive home with us, the chickens creep silently and fearfully about, afraid of their own shadows. They have to be lifted into their secure bed time coop, and shown where the 'have an egg' boxes are.

They have no idea that lettuce, sunflower seeds, and meal worms are edible and yummy, and they don't realise that they can simply wander in and out of their shed as they please.

In short, they are living and breathing, but little else.

Until, that is, they realise that they have retired to chicken heaven, and explode into natural chicken activity!

Within a week the little lost souls blossom into bright, active, nosey, bundles of feathers, spending their time digging deep holes, foraging, running about, and eating.

They are a joy to watch.

The chickens usually change their feathers once they have settled in to their new lives, and thereby become even more beautiful.

We named one very small chicken 'Scraggy', because although she grew her new feathers everywhere else, her neck remained bald. That particular part of her looked as though it should have been in a freezer in Tesco.

But she made up for this lack of plumage by developing into one of the biggest characters in the flock. She spent the greater part of each day running around, darting here and there, usually from one food source to another, and eating as if the food itself was going out of fashion.

Whenever I went into their enclosure she would follow me about, watching what I was doing, wondering if I was the bearer of anything edible, and she would always accompany me into the small shed when I cleaned it out. She would take the opportunity to help herself to as much food from the dish by the door in there as she could cram in, eating so fast that her beak tap tapped on the side of the dish.

Considering how much she ate every day it is something of a miracle that she remained so small.

Not many months ago Tod came back in after giving the chickens their breakfast, and opening up the sheds to let them out.

He told me that one of them had died overnight. I was devastated. We usually manage to get any sick chicken to the Vet's in time, but they are secretive about illness, and I had obviously missed this one. Although are very fond of each and every chicken in our care, we do have our favourites, and when Tod told me that it was Scraggy who had died, I was really upset. I would miss her and her funny little ways. She was a huge character.

Late afternoon the same day I went out to the chicken enclosure to clean the sheds. I went straight into the small one, and started to open the boxes and clean up, my back to the door.

My mind was far away from what I was doing. I was wondering what shopping I needed, and if I would have time to get it later.

It was probably because, over the months, I had grown so used to that particular sound accompanying my efforts to clean out the boxes, that it didn't immediately register with me. Although the quick tap tapping on the dish by the door had been going on for at least a couple of minutes, it was only then that I realised I shouldn't have been hearing it.

I whipped round and stared at the food dish.

'Scraggy' was standing in it, eating for England.

Oh wow! I thought. I can see her perfectly clearly! That's amazing!

I was stunned at just how sharp and clear Scraggy's image was. It didn't waver, and it wasn't obscured by mist or movement across it. I wondered if my mediumistic ability had taken a turn for the better!

I was mesmerised by this crystal clear vision, and slowly stepped closer, and dropped to my knees to see it better.

'Scraggy' paid me no attention, but continued to do what she had always done in life; eat!

Curious, I wondered if I would be able to touch her, to feel her feathers, and so slowly and carefully, holding my breath, I reached out towards her.

My fingertips brushed her wing. She stopped eating and raised her head. There was a moment of absolute stillness, of awe and wonder, and then she turned and pecked my hand hard.

Hummm, I thought, somewhat miffed, this is probably *not* a Spirit Scraggy! That could well account for the clarity of the vision, and the red mark on my hand.

Sure enough, Tod had muddled Scraggy with another little chicken, but one which had rather more feathers on her neck.

Scraggy remains here to this day, and can of course be found cramming her beak with food at every possible opportunity.

"For the soul of every living thing is in the hand of God."
Job 12:10

Chapter Nine

Joan

Tod's mother became ill around about Christmas time a couple of years ago. By April the illness had been diagnosed as stomach cancer, and we knew she didn't have long.

She came to stay with us. Although Tod and I had been together for a long time, I hadn't seen a great deal of his mother Joan over the years, and in many ways I didn't really know her at all.

The four months that she spent with us, the last four months of her life, was a heart wrenching time for Tod. He loved his mother dearly.

Joan and I got to know each other over that time, and as spring became a warm summer, we became friends.

Emotionally she was an immensely strong woman, and she dealt with her dreadful illness, the horrendous symptoms and pain, and the all too quick and unexpected approach of her death, with immeasurable fortitude. She was braver than the brave. I grew to respect and admire her.

Joan knew that she would have another life when she passed over, and she often asked me about the Spirit World. I answered her questions as best I could, sometimes giving her books to read, to add to what I was able to tell her.

She was looking forward to meeting up again with her younger sister who had died suddenly only the year before, and she was expecting to see her mother and grandmother waiting at her bedside just before she passed.

"They'll show me the way to go, will they?" she asked me.

"I think they certainly will," I told her. "You don't need to worry about that."

The large number of family and friends who came to visit Joan over that period was testament to her widespread popularity. She was much loved.

Another of her sisters, Connie, came to stay with us for a few weeks, to help with Joan's nursing care.

We put a bed downstairs in the conservatory for Connie, and as Joan's condition worsened, Connie would often get up in the night, walk through the back room, along the hallway and into the front room to check on Joan there.

In the early hours of one morning I lay wide awake, listening to the sound of complete silence in the house, staring through the impenetrable darkness, wondering what the future would bring. I had just been downstairs to see how Joan was. She had reached that vague netherworld between sleep and unconsciousness, and had not moved at all for hours.

Suddenly there was a loud shout. It startled me both by its unexpectedness and by the volume of the sound. It had filled the whole house. It was just one shouted word, but I didn't know what that word was. Tod sat up in bed next to me, "What was that?" he said. "Who was shouting?"

We both got up and hurried downstairs to make sure Joan had not been disturbed. As we reached the hallway, Connie was just walking quickly through from the back room. She was shaken.

"What was that?" she asked. "Was that you shouting?"

Interestingly enough we had all heard the shout, and we had all heard it as just one single word, but none of us knew what that word was. We didn't know either, if it had been a man's voice or a woman's.

Joan remained unmoving, undisturbed.

This kind of sudden, loud shout, or unidentifiable noise, is not uncommon in the environment of someone who is gravely ill, and within hours or days of passing over. But the jury is out about the precise reason for the shout, although most would agree that it comes directly from the Spirit World. I feel that it may be a form of reassurance for those whose loved one is dying, as the sound is almost invariably heard by everyone present, even those who have never before heard a Spirit voice.

The following day the wonderfully caring Minister from the local Hospice came to see Joan. She (the Minister is a woman) spent an hour alone with her, and when she had gone Joan told me, in a weak, breathless whisper, some of what had been said, and asked me to explain if I could.

I eventually realised that the Minister had read a well-known poem to Joan; a beautiful, touching, comforting explanatory poem. I found a copy of it, and read it to Joan again. This is it:

What is Dying

I am standing upon that foreshore; a ship at my side spreads her white sails to the morning breeze and starts for the blue ocean.

She is an object of beauty and strength, and I stand and watch her until at length she hangs like a speck of white cloud just where the sea and sky come down to mingle with each other. Then someone at my side says,

"There! She's gone!"

"Gone where?"

"Gone from my sight, that's all".

She is just as large in mast and spar and hull as ever she was when she left my side; just as able to bear her load of living freight to the place of her destination.

Her diminished size is in me, not in her.

And just at that moment when someone at my side says,
"There! She's gone!"
There are other eyes watching her coming, and other
voices ready to take up the glad shout,
"Here she comes!"
And that is dying.

By/Attributed to Bishop Brent

"Ah," Joan said quietly, as I finished reading, "So I'm a ship,
am I?" and we both giggled.

Tod spent a lot of time over the last couple of weeks of
Joan's life sitting with his mother as she lay in bed, holding
her hand, and chatting to her when she was awake. Later that
day, with Joan's condition rapidly worsening, Tod asked me
if I was aware of any Spirit people in the room.

He knows that my motto has always been, 'When I'm
working, I'm working; but when I'm *not* working, don't ask
me, because I won't tell you!'

However, if ever there was a right time to make an
exception to my rule, this was it. So I told him that there
were, in fact, two very bright Spirit lights at the top of Joan's
bed. They had been there, on and off, for a number of days. I
didn't know who they were; I saw them only as lights.

There was also a man standing at the foot of her bed. He
was tall, dressed in dark clothing, and seemed to have quite
long, untidy hair. I had seen him there on a number of
occasions. Again, I didn't know who he was.

Tod continued to sit with Joan into the early evening that
day, as she drifted in and out of consciousness. The nurses
came and went. The doctor visited. At one point she opened
her eyes and whispered to Tod, "Is that mother?" and then,
"Is that my mother and grandmother standing behind you?"

And later on she asked, "Who is that man?" as she stared
towards the end of her bed.

76

I came downstairs that night, and found Tod sitting next to the bed, holding Joan's hand in both of his. She had just died.

"The death of a mother is the first sorrow wept without her."
Unknown author.

Chapter Ten

Dior

From the mid nineteen seventies until the mid nineteen eighties I was lucky enough to live and work in that wonderfully elegant, vibrant and exciting city, Paris.

I just loved the time I spent there. I loved the people, I loved the language, and I loved the way of life. As a Teacher of English as a Foreign Language, which was quite a rare commodity in Paris at that time, interesting doors would frequently open for my colleagues and me, and we were invited to any number of parties, art exhibitions, restaurants, night clubs and shows on a regular basis. Life was wonderfully full and exciting.

I taught English to business people in their places of work, and spent several years teaching regularly in a number of companies. One of those was Christian Dior.

If I remember rightly the Christian Dior Boutique was in Avenue Montaigne, at street level, and many of the Dior fashion workshops and admin offices were located in the building directly above it.

I remember walking into the Boutique on my first day there carrying my books, paper and pens in a plastic supermarket carrier bag, a wildly inappropriate item to import into the sumptuous, classy environment in which I found myself!

I taught the staff who worked in the Boutique, and also several people employed in the specialised dress and hat making departments.

They were some of the nicest, kindest, most amusing people I have ever met, and they treated me as if I were a member of the Dior staff, one of the extended Dior family. I loved every minute of my time there.

One particularly warm early spring day, when Paris was beginning to look beautiful again, after months of gloom imposed on that gorgeous city by a long, cold winter of winds and rain, I arrived at the Boutique in good time for the English classes.

I still remember the wonderfully evocative, alluring fragrance that permeated the Boutique. It reminded me of a mixture of expensive perfume and clean, fresh linen, and washed gently over you the moment you stepped across the threshold, and the door closed silently behind you on the world outside. That subtle fragrance alerted the senses, and reminded and reassured you that you had entered the rarefied world of Dior haute couture.

Two of my 'students' were standing at the back of the Boutique that day, beside the door which led out into the hallway, and from which access could be gained to the floors above. They greeted me warmly, held the door open for me, and then followed me out into the hallway.

One of the ladies worked in the specialised dress making department, "The dress is finished," she told me excitedly. "Everything is done."

I knew exactly what she was talking about. Some mention had been made during every class over the last month about *'the dress'*. All the staff knew about that particular, mysterious garment, and had followed its progress eagerly on a daily basis.

It was a wedding dress, designed and created for the much loved daughter of a particularly wealthy family from the Middle East, and it was like no other dress anyone had ever seen. It was made of layer upon layer of the finest, exquisite silk, and was hand sewn with hundreds of the highest quality pearls and diamonds. It was obviously extremely valuable, and was kept under constant lock and key in the Dior building.

"We'll show you. You must see it. It is incredible," the ladies said now. Their enthusiasm was infectious and I grinned. "I'd love to," I said.

"We have the keys to the back door of the workshop. If you go up the stairs here," and they indicated the magnificent marble staircase that I was standing beside, "to the very top, we will go round and open the door there for you." They hurried off together, two immaculately dressed and impeccably coiffed Dior ladies, down a corridor towards a small wooden door which they unlocked, opened, and then disappeared through, leaving me to begin the climb up the spiralling marble stairs alone.

A heavy hush permeated the building. There was no one else around. My high heels click clacked on the shiny cream coloured marble of the stairs, the sound echoing around the high walls and out into the spacious stairwell. Occasionally I reached out to touch the wooden surface of the black painted wrought iron bannister rail that snaked all the way up to the top beside the stairs, its ornate scrolls and rose patterns glinting as they caught the light.

It felt rather strange to be there alone, a lowly English teacher, in that lovely old building that housed some of the world's most creative minds in the genre of fashion.

I climbed upwards, further and further, and soon my thoughts drifted far away from the Dior building, and danced fleetingly from one thing to another. Eventually I focused on the English lesson to come. I wondered how it would go, and if all the 'students' would be able to attend. Did I have enough photocopies of the magazine article I intended reading and discussing with them? Had I remembered to bring a few extra with me?

I rounded what I now saw was the final bend in the staircase, and started on the last stretch upwards. I watched my feet, and silently counted the steps as I went.

Aware that I was beginning to feel slightly out of breath I glanced up, checking how much further I had to go, and hoping it wasn't too far. But suddenly I gasped in amazement and stopped where I was, jolted into immobility, with one foot in mid-air in front of me, poised to ascend the next stair.

My brain could not immediately assimilate what I saw, and for a moment I was in danger of wobbling off the step and slipping downwards. I grabbed the handrail to steady myself.

There, maybe ten or twelve stairs above me stood a beautiful young woman wearing a dress that could only have come straight out of the pages of a child's fantasy story. It shone and shimmered, falling in soft, gleaming layers around her body, and down to her feet, as if it were permeated by small, bright Christmas lights. Surely only a Fairy Godmother would wear such a dress.

I blinked, and she was gone, that beautiful young woman with the soulful, tragic expression on her face.

I was stunned, and stood completely still, unwilling to move on, staring up towards the top of the staircase, trying to put my thoughts in order, feeling slightly dazed, and wondering what on earth I had just seen.

There was suddenly a loud jingling and metallic scraping sound from above me, and with quite a screech the door at the very top of the staircase opened.

"Come in! Come in!" my two 'students' called to me as they appeared round the door, smiling and beckoning.

I took a deep breath, walked quickly up the last few steps and followed them into the workshop. They closed and locked the door behind me, and then walked over to a very large window half way down the room. This was the source of natural light in the workshop, necessary to enable any hand sewing to take place.

"Here it is!" they said, rolling back a heavy bamboo screen below the window to reveal *'the dress'* behind it, adorning a mannequin.

It was stunning, exquisite and breath-taking, and I had already seen it.

It was the same dress that the beautiful, tragic young woman had been wearing outside on the staircase just a few moments before.

"Oh how beautiful!" I said, and it truly was.

Wearing pristine cotton gloves the ladies lifted several sections of the dress and showed me how the diamonds and pearls had been sew onto it. I was impressed. It was a totally spectacular garment, of which they were rightly proud.

I could not get the vision of that young woman on the Dior stairs, wearing the beautiful, fairy tale dress, out of my mind. For the next few days I thought of little else. I didn't understand it. Who was the woman I had seen? Had the dress been made for her? Why did she appear to be so very sad? I just didn't have any answers.

The following week I was working again at the Dior Boutique. The last class of the day included some of the ladies from the specialised dressmaking department, and at the end of the class, when the others had left the room, I sat chatting to the two ladies who had shown me *the dress*. Eventually, during a break in the conversation, I asked them if it had been collected yet, or had it been sent abroad?

There was a sudden, unaccustomed silence in the room, and the ladies exchanged glances. They seemed uncomfortable, and they shrugged their shoulders and looked down at their books and papers on the table in front of them. It was obvious that my question had touched some kind of nerve, and they didn't seem able, or willing, to answer me.

I felt awkward, and started to collect my pens and papers together, not knowing what else to do, wondering what to say, how to escape from this embarrassing situation that I had unwittingly created.

A difficult minute passed. Eventually, "It has been destroyed," one of the ladies said in a voice so low as to be hardly audible, "the staff were ordered to destroy *the dress* yesterday, and so they did." She shook her head. She looked completely dejected.

"What!" I exclaimed, unable to keep the shock out of my voice, "Why? What on earth happened?"

"We do not know," they said, "We think there was some kind of catastrophe, but we do not know for sure. We will probably never know. "

I continued to teach at Dior for another two years. *The dress*, and the strange, sad fate that befell it, was never mentioned again.

Chapter Eleven

The Tudor House

Not long after I had left France for good and set up home in Folkestone, England, I took a phone call from the director of my 'old' English language school in Paris.

"Can you do a residential course for us?" he asked me, "It's just down the coast from you, not far away. It's only for a week."

So, in bright summer sunshine, a few days later, I found myself sitting in a taxi as it drove down a winding, tree lined path, through undeniably perfect gardens laid by Capability Brown, towards the magnificent Tudor house where I was to spend a week teaching English to a small group of French business men.

The house was owned by a private family who had been persuaded to host a number of English Language 'students' there during the summer. It was a truly wonderful, original and completely preserved Tudor house, dating from the early 1500s.

I arrived there late afternoon on a warm day in August, when I suppose the house and gardens probably looked at their very best. I was completely smitten on first sight. It was stunning.

Anna, the elegant, beautifully dressed, middle aged lady of the house, showed me round, and told me something of its impressive history. It was large, situated in a prime position on the south coast, and had been visited by many of royal and noble birth over the centuries.

We walked along corridors which seemed to go on and on as they wound through different wings of the house, up and down curving wooden staircases, and eventually into the great hall, which was now a beautifully appointed dining room. And through it all, at every vantage point, the green and pleasant rolling gardens were visible from the clusters of tall windows scattered strategically around the house.

"The girls are here," my hostess said, pointing out of one of the windows towards a fenced off area of grass which seemed much taller than the rest. A group of white and fluffy sheep were just streaming out of a trailer parked at the gate, and setting to munching the grass.

"They're our lawn mowers!" she said, grinning, "We borrow them every summer." And she waved to the farmer who was closing up the trailer and preparing to leave again, having delivered his cargo of four legged grass trimmers.

"Come on," she said, "I'll show you to your room. It's in the West wing." And we set off towards a part of the house I had not yet seen.

At the top of the main staircase we turned down a long, narrow corridor which, having just one small window in its complete length, was now only dimly lit. The air around us seemed to be full of moving, circling dark shadows, and as we walked, my high heels clicking on the highly polished old floorboards, I felt the hairs on the back of my neck move slightly. I was uneasy there.

"Here we are," Anna said, stopping in front of an old wooden door, the surface of which was criss crossed with metal bands that looked as if they were original Tudor. She lifted the heavy metal latch and pushed. The door swung open revealing a large room, with very little furniture in it.

"You won't be disturbed in here," she said, walking into the room and over to the window that overlooked part of the gardens. "You're the only one in this wing. It's very quiet."

"Thank you," I said, "I'm sure I'll be fine here. It's lovely."

We chatted for a few moments and then Anna said, "See you for dinner at seven." She walked back across the room and out the door, closing it softly behind her.

Left alone I spent a while gazing out the window, enjoying the enchanting view, and marvelling at the fact that there had been hardly any change in it since the house was built so long ago. Who had stood where I was now standing, looking out where I was now looking? What had they been thinking?

It was indeed a large room. Apart from the bed and bedside table, a sink, and a small wardrobe and table, it was empty. My footsteps echoed across the wooden floor, bouncing off the ancient ceiling beams. I opened the door onto the corridor and walked across to check out the bathroom there, making sure I knew where it was.

As I walked back, and pushed the door to my room open, a clock chimed behind me on the corridor. I jumped. I hadn't noticed any clock. I looked further along the corridor through the increasing dimness there, and could just about make out a grandfather clock standing against the wall. It was still chiming; a loud, deep, penetrating, but not unpleasant sound that filled the whole corridor.

I started to walk along to have a look at the clock, but stopped. Somehow I just didn't feel I wanted to do that. A chill touched my neck, and I went back into my room and closed the door.

I went down for dinner in good time and met the 'students' who had all arrived by then. We had a very pleasant meal, together with our host family. Everyone was rather shy and quiet, but I had no doubt that after a few days that would change, and we would all get along really well, once the 'students' had gained a bit of confidence in their use of English.

Later on I said goodnight, and started on my way back to my room. I had some preparation to do for the classes the next day.

"Oh, just a moment Fiona," Anna called, "can I have a word?"

I turned and waited for her, and we stood together at the bottom of the staircase.

"I just thought I'd better mention something to you about the West wing corridor, the one your room's on," she said, smiling at me.

"The corridor?" I said. "Oh, OK; what about it?"

"Well, you see…." she said, hesitating slightly. I waited, wondering what was coming. "It's haunted," she said.

"*Is* it?" I said, "How wonderful!" And I grinned at her.

"Oh, I'm so glad you're alright about it!" She sounded relieved. "We've actually had one or two friends staying over the years who were absolutely terrified. We had to move them to another wing," she said, smiling at me. "Are you *sure* you'll be OK?"

"Oh don't worry about *me*," I told her. "There's no way I'd be terrified of a ghost! In fact I can't wait to see it. Who is it, do you know?"

"Yes, we've had one or two researchers here from time to time to check on it, and the ghost seems to be a nobleman who owned the house in Tudor times. He turned against the King and was executed in one purge or another, I don't remember which, but apparently he had his private rooms over in the west wing."

"How interesting!" I said. This was looking really good.

"Yes," Anna said. "After his death the house was given to a friend of the King's as a reward for his loyalty."

"Well, well," I said. "So when does the nobleman walk?"

"On the stroke of midnight he comes from the main staircase along the corridor and past the room where you are," Anna told me. "He walks as far as the grandfather clock and then disappears."

"Do you know *why* he walks along there?" I asked.

"Apparently he's looking for vengeance," she said, smiling sweetly. "Looking for members of the family who took the house from him."

For the first time in the conversation I *didn't* feel like smiling. Humm, 'looking for vengeance' had quite a ring to it, didn't it? A feather of fright touched the back of my neck.

I sat up in bed and read a book by the light of the small bedside lamp. I found it hard to concentrate on the pages because I was excited, looking forward to coming face to face with a ghost. I had decided that as soon as the clock began chiming I would get up and open the bedroom door, and wait for the ghost to come along the corridor. I would have a great view, as 'he' would pass right by me.

The room looked even bigger as darkness reached in through the window, and grotesque, looming shadows seemed to move about at the end of the bed, jostling for position, watching me closely, waiting for their opportunity to pounce.

There was complete and absolute, heavy silence inside the ancient house. It pressed down on me, and eventually I set aside my book and stared wide eyed and unseeing into the pitch black void, watching, listening, and waiting.

An owl screeched sharply outside, somewhere above the darkened, empty gardens, and I jumped. A floorboard creaked suddenly in the gloom across the room – what was that? Was someone or some*thing* in the room? Watching me? Creeping towards me? Waiting to get me? I suddenly felt very isolated and alone.

My breathing grew quicker, shallower, and my palms became sweaty. I swear my hair began to stand on end. I told myself to calm down, to be sensible. This was a ghost, only a ghost, not something that could actually hurt me….

When finally the old grandfather clock began to strike the hour of midnight I wanted to scream in fright. I held my breath and counted the deep, resounding chimes. Twelve came and went, and I could have cried with relief as there was a sudden silence, and no other sound around. Nothing. No ghost. No walking, spooky spectre. I managed a smile. How stupid I had been to be so scared!

I reached out a shaky hand and put the bedside lamp off, and settled down to sleep.

The footsteps were heavy and measured. I thought at first it was the grandfather clock winding itself up to strike again. But it wasn't, of course. It was the heavy tread of ancient feet coming towards my room; ancient feet clad in equally ancient leather boots. I could hear a slight jingle with every step, as if a buckle on the boots was loose, and the old wooden floorboards of the corridor creaked and moved beneath 'his' weight.

They came nearer and nearer, growing louder and louder as 'he' approached the bedroom door.

I dived into a trembling, blind panic, and threw myself under the bedclothes, pulling them over my head, blocking out the sound of those approaching spectral footsteps, of that vengeance seeking phantom step- stepping along the corridor towards me. *Nothing* on this earth would have persuaded me to take a peek out of the bedroom door.

I might have slept for a couple of hours that night. I don't remember now.

I do remember though how much I enjoyed the week, and I was sorry to leave, to say goodbye to that wonderful house in its stunning setting, and to some very congenial people.

I didn't listen out for the ghost after that first night, and I didn't hear 'him' again. Thank goodness!

Back home, where my friends of course knew of my particular interest in Spiritualism and the Paranormal, I quickly became the centre of a great deal of amusement when I admitted that I had had a marvellous chance to see a ghost up close, *very* close, but had blown it, and chickened out, because when it came to it I was far too scared!

All these years on, and so much water has passed under the bridge, but my friends have still not forgotten the 'night of the spectral footsteps'! And neither have I!

*For a full explanation of what a ghost really is, and how it differs from a Spirit person, please see my previous book, **'Voices'**.

Chapter Twelve

It's *YOU!*

Last year Tod opened the door to my ten o'clock reading. It was a cold day; the temperature was hovering around freezing, so I wasn't going to be working in Todington Lodge, out in the garden. I was already sitting in the sensibly very warm lounge, waiting for my client.

I heard her greeting Tod in rather a loud, unfamiliar voice, heard the front door close, and then the lounge door was flung open, and a woman appeared in the doorway. She stopped there, one hand still on the door handle, only a step or two into the room, and stared over at me.

I stood up, smiled at her, and said, "Hello, take a seat."

I was immediately aware that I did not know her. I had never met her before, and knew nothing at all about her, except the mobile number she had given me when making this appointment. That was quite usual.

But instead of moving across to the sofa and sitting down there, my visitor remained standing where she was, staring hard at me, a quizzical expression on her face.

My initial impression of the woman was that she was larger than life, brimming with confidence, and would probably be the life and soul of any party you care to mention.

I repeated, "Take a seat," gesturing towards the sofa and smiling at her.

Suddenly, "It *is* you!" she almost shouted, "It really *is* you!" And throwing her head back she followed up that rather peculiar assertion with a loud and somewhat manic giggle.

I was taken aback, not just by the volume of her voice, which filled the room, and possibly the room next door too, but also by what she was saying. I didn't understand what she meant.

"It's *you!*" she said, "Fiona, it's *you!*" And she giggled again.

I stared blankly at her, "What do you mean?" I asked. "You'll have to explain, I'm afraid. I don't know what you're talking about."

I sat down, hoping that this distinctly odd woman would take the hint and sit down herself, but she didn't. Instead she began walking around the room, stopping every so often to repeat, "It's *you!* It really *is you!*" giggling and pointing agitatedly at me.

I was mystified and astonished, in equal parts.

"OK," I said, as calmly as I could manage. "Please take a seat and tell me what you mean."

"You *know!* You *know!*" she said. "It *is* you!" She appeared to have no intention of sitting down.

I started to feel distinctly annoyed, and somewhere in my brain a little voice began to mutter something about possible mental health issues. "Look!" I said firmly, "If you don't sit down and tell me what you're talking about you'll have to leave!"

"But it's *you!*" she screeched, dashing over to the sofa and sitting down on it. "It's *you!*"

She appeared to think that if she was sitting down I wouldn't be able to eject her from the room. I was glad that Tod was in the house, in case I needed some help. The lounge door was still partially open, and I wondered if he could hear what was going on.

"Well, tell me then," I said. "What are you talking about?"

"You *know*!" she said, rather more quietly than before, but there wasn't much in it. A note of petulance had crept into her voice now.

"*If* I knew what you were talking about I'd *tell* you," I said. "But I don't. So I'm sorry, but if you don't explain yourself you'll have to leave." I was really annoyed now, and didn't mind letting her know that.

"You *must* remember me!" she said, leaning forward and clasping her hands together on her lap. "I've been here to this house before. I've *met* you before."

I looked at her. She was probably getting on for fifty years old. She had short, dark brown, wavy hair and a pleasant face. I saw in front of me a woman who I had never met before. I did not know her, and I told her that.

Her reaction was startling. "You *have* met me before! You *know* me! I've been *here* before!" she positively boomed, glaring at me.

I shook my head. "OK. That's enough!" I said. "I would like you to leave now please," and I stood up and started to move towards the door.

"It was when you were with your ex-husband," she said, "I came here with my mother and we had a cup of tea with you both." And she stared at me, smiling and nodding her head expectantly, waiting for me to 'remember' the occasion.

But I didn't. Because it wasn't *me* she had met.

The first time I left my ex-husband, following the revelation that he had propositioned the dental receptionist while I was actually in the surgery next door, having treatment, I went back to the south of England, where I had lived previously, and still had friends.

The next day he moved his latest girlfriend, just one in a constant stream of extra marital women, into our house. I had never met this one, but I had been told by a number of different people, on several occasions, that we looked very similar. That similarity was in fact so marked that I once took a phone call from someone who couldn't understand why I was at home, and answering the phone, when she had just seen 'me' twenty five miles away at a show hosted by my ex-husband.

Of course, it wasn't *me*! But it *was* the girlfriend who later moved into my house for a short time.

So, I attempted to explain to the woman who was sitting on my sofa grinning at me, that she had not met *me* when she came to the house, but it had in fact been my ex-husband's latest girlfriend who she met, a girlfriend who happened to closely resemble me.

The woman clearly did not believe me. Her grin disappeared and she stared at me. Her voice took on an unpleasant edge of sarcasm, "Oh well, if you say so," she said, "we may as well start the reading now."

Given the circumstances the most sensible thing to do would have been to show the woman out then. But for some reason I didn't. I was irritated; annoyed that this woman thought I was lying to her; heaven only knew why I would be doing that; and the whole situation obviously affected my judgement.

I started a reading. It was the worst possible thing I could have done.

My concentration was lacking, I felt uncomfortable and out of sorts.

That was probably why I didn't immediately identify the Spirit entity that had built up in the corner of the room.

However, I did know what the connection was to my rather odd client, so, "Your mother is here," I told the woman. But I suddenly felt certain that it was all useless, and that no matter what I did or said, this reading would be fatally flawed.

"Well, you *do* know her," the woman said in a flat, vaguely accusatory voice. "You've met her enough times."

"She's not giving me her name, or showing me any way of identifying her," I said, "I don't know who she is."

It is of course not the case that every Spirit visitation is readily identifiable. The appearance of a Spirit entity falls at any point along a broad spectrum, from bright and clearly definable at one end, to nebulous, misty and vague at the other.

Sometimes I see only a ball of sharp, bright, and clearly defined light, hovering in front of me at about chest height, rather like a shining tennis ball. But at other times I can only make out a vague, shapeless, dull light.

I may sometimes be lucky enough to see a bright light which then transforms into a figure, but of course, as I have already said, the clarity of that figure may be situated anywhere along a spectrum from crisp and sharp at one end, right through to nebulous, or hazy and ill-defined at the other.

A Spirit visitor will usually say something, or highlight something, some kind of clue, to facilitate recognition. If this does not happen the Medium will often be left floundering through metaphorical mud, wondering what to say next.

And that was exactly what happened to me in this case. The vague and hazy figure of a woman standing unmoving in the corner of the room did not give me any pointer at all as to her identity, that is, until she said, "Shirley."

And I knew instantly who she was. It was not a happy revelation.

Several years prior to this memorable reading I was alone one afternoon in the Psychic Centre which I ran with my ex-husband. It was very quiet; no events were booked in until the evening, so I had taken the opportunity to sort through some paperwork without being disturbed. It lay in a pile on the table in front of me.

But after only a short time I heard the street door downstairs rattle open, followed by the sound of someone slowly and laboriously climbing the stairs. My peace and quiet was about to be interrupted.

The woman who eventually appeared, puffing and panting, at the door of the Centre, had struggled to climb the stairs up to it. She was considerably overweight.

I knew her name, as she attended the Centre fairly regularly, but I had never spoken to her, and knew little or nothing about her.

"Hello Shirley," I said now, as she walked slowly across the room towards me. She didn't respond, and I wondered if she was slightly deaf. "Have a seat and get your breath back," I said, "those stairs are quite steep."

But she simply looked at me, with what I might describe as a less than welcoming expression on her face, and continued walking until she reached the other side of the table I was working at. She stopped there and stared at me, her head slightly cocked to one side, as if she was assessing me in some way.

I waited, curious, wondering what she wanted, and why she was there at that time of day.

"You should be ashamed of yourself," she said, her voice loud and harsh, the Scottish accent very pronounced; and she narrowed her eyes and glared at me, "That poor man. He tries his best to look after you, but all you can do is spend his money, and sit about drinking expensive wine and doing nothing all day!"

It was *my* turn to stare. I was flabbergasted. "What on earth are you talking about?" I said, feeling the blood rush to my cheeks, turning them hot instantly.

"You know exactly what I'm talking about," she said, "Billy has told me everything. You've practically ruined his life. He's even asked me for a loan because you've spent every penny he has!" And she made a strange noise in her throat that sounded like half sneer and half tut.

96

"Do you know what," I said as calmly as I could, "you really don't have a clue! In fact, you have no idea at all!" I was angry, angry and upset.

"I know what Billy told me!" she said, and turned and started to walk away towards the door, her mission, as she saw it, successfully completed. I watched as she disappeared down the corridor, and then I heard her heavy footsteps descending the stairs. She slammed the door as she left.

I was devastated. I had already taken a couple of steps along the road to separation and divorce, and I was becoming aware of my then husband's propensity to tell odd and unflattering, made-up stories about me. But I was still finding that hard to believe, and even harder to accept. However, here was yet another person who had heard those made-up stories, and who believed them.

As the sun slanted in through the windows of the Psychic Centre, sending little shadows creeping across my unfinished paperwork in front of me, I sat alone in the silence and cried.

A few days later Shirley and a friend came out of a local shop, as Billy and I were parked alongside the pavement in the car.

Spotting him she called, "Good on you Billy!" in a loud, defiant voice, and she opened the car door and attempted to embrace him.

I can only assume that she wanted to underline the fact that she believed what he had told her about me, rather than the evidence of her own eyes.

Those words were the last I ever heard from Shirley, as I left my husband just a matter of weeks later, following my chat with the Citizens Band Radio gentleman. I moved, for a while, far away from the area.

But the desperate unhappiness and helplessness of that epoch remains etched on my memory to this day, so it was something of an unpleasant shock to find myself, last year, once again face to face with Shirley, even though this time she was across the divide, in the Spirit World.

There was absolutely no way I could begin to achieve any meaningful communication with her. She knew that. It was never going to happen.

So I ended the reading, the reading that I should never have started in the first place. I should have paid attention to my own instincts.

Chapter Thirteen

Dogs

I didn't know the pleasant looking middle aged woman who stood smiling uncertainly at me through the somewhat dusty glass of our porch door. She had arrived exactly on time for her reading, and had rung the doorbell at 10am precisely.

I stepped from the hall down into the small porch, reached out and started to pull the front door open to let her in, but it had always been awkward, and now it stuck fast.

"Sorry!" I called to her, "The stupid door's stuck again!" and I yanked hard on the handle, as my embarrassment with the situation sent the blood racing to my cheeks. But the door refused to budge.

The woman grinned at me through the window. "I'll give it a push!" she called, and immediately did so with gusto. The unexpected force with which the door thwacked me sent me tottering backwards, and the red painted, hitherto innocuous step up into the hall suddenly whipped my lower legs out from under me as they crashed into it. With nothing to grab on to to keep me upright I sat down heavily on the hall floor, and only just prevented the onset of that ridiculous pantomime situation of my legs shooting up into the air, while I thrashed about like a fish out of water, trying to right myself again.

Oddly enough I remember thinking I was glad to be wearing jeans.

My client stood looking down at me, an entirely unembarrassed smile on her face. I looked up at her and shook my head, grinning sheepishly.

"I don't think I've ever made an entrance like *that*!" she said, and we both laughed.

"And I don't think I've ever greeted a client in such an unprofessional manner!" I said, as she helped me upright. I rubbed my scraped elbow ruefully.

"The reading's bound to be a let-down after that!" I told her, and she smiled at me. I knew I liked her, this stranger, and I knew immediately that she was here for a particular reason. She had not come to ask about her love life or prospects of promotion at work. She had something much more serious on her mind.

We settled ourselves in my room, she on the sofa opposite me, and I began the reading.

Within minutes a small bright light in the corner of the room caught my eye. The white, glowing Spirit light grew rapidly in size, and I became aware of a figure building up there. It was a man, standing absolutely still, staring at the woman.

Although his form was largely indistinct, he appeared to be dressed entirely in dark blue. Then I noticed a large dog sitting close beside his leg. It too remained absolutely still, also staring at the woman.

Although the dog's form was out of focus to me and considerably blurred, I was sure it was an Alsatian or German shepherd, and it was indeed very large.

I had the sudden, bizarre impression that I was looking at a statue of a man and dog, rather than Spirit entities, and I opened my mouth meaning to tell the woman my thoughts, but before I could do so the man moved.

He turned his head in my direction, and I somehow knew he was waiting for me to speak.

I did so, telling the woman what I could see, describing the man, and adding that he was wearing dark blue clothes, maybe some kind of work clothes or even a uniform.

She sat in silence, watching me, listening intently. When I mentioned the dog the woman nodded, and for the first time during the reading so far a smile appeared on her face.

"Yes," she said, "that's his dog, his special dog. They loved each other. Went everywhere together."

And then finally the man spoke, slowly and indistinctly. My visitor was his wife, he told me, and they had not been married very long when an illness had caused his death. There were some personal details that he wanted to pass on to her, and then he said, "Thank her for putting it in the coffin. She did the right thing. It was really thoughtful of her."

The woman stared at me in silence when I told her what he had said. She stared for so long that I wondered if I had got it wrong, misunderstood in some way, or misinterpreted what the man wanted to say.

"I know people often put personal items in coffins with their loved ones, but you put something **very** unusual, **very** special in the coffin with him," I said, hoping to clarify things, "and he wants to thank you for that. You must have had some doubts about whether you had done the right thing?"

"Yes," she said quietly, "I did. I really wasn't sure if I'd done something stupid. I've been really worried about it."

"Well, I don't know what it was that you put in with him, but as I say, he's pleased," I said, "so you certainly did the right thing."

"It was his dog," the woman said quickly, "His dog had died just before my husband did, and so I put him in the coffin. I sent them off together."

"Oh wow! How lovely!" I said, "No wonder he's pleased."

Some months later the woman came back to see me.

We giggled about the entrance she had made on her first visit to my house. This time she made a more conventional one.

After exchanging pleasantries I began the reading and almost immediately her husband appeared. He was wearing the same dark blue clothes as I had seen him in the first time.

And the big dog was with him, sitting, as before, close to his leg.

"The last one has just arrived," he said very clearly, addressing his wife.

"I've no idea what he means," I told her, "Is he talking about something in the post maybe?"

"No," she said, grinning, "I know exactly what he's talking about. He used to train dogs, and he loved them all. They were very special to him. All but one of his dogs died before *he* did.

But that one, the very last dog, has just died. So that's what he means. The 'last one' has just arrived over in the Spirit World. He's got all his dogs with him now. He'll be so happy."

"Until one has loved an animal, a part of one's soul
remains unawakened."
Anatole France.

102

Chapter Fourteen

Buddy

This chapter is considerably longer than usual. I feel that its content merits the increased length, and I hope that you, the reader, will understand that.

The following is dedicated to all those of us who have ever loved a dog.

**

We were shocked when Kate told us she was thinking of emigrating to Australia.

"But you *can't*!" Donna and I said indignantly, "Australia's too far to go for dinner! We'd never get back in time for work the next morning!"

We all giggled, but a fragile, uncertain silence descended on the three of us, and we stared at Kate across the small, round restaurant table that was crammed to overflowing with cutlery, condiments, menus and wine glasses, waiting for her to tell us she was only joking; *hoping* she would tell us that she was only joking.

"Sorry, Girlies," Kate said quietly, "we've already made the decision; we're emigrating."

My initial shock at hearing Kate's life changing news turned instantly to excitement for her. How wonderful! How thrilling! A new start in life, with all the marvellous opportunities that moving to Australia would bring.

Kate, Donna and I had become friends at work; well, at a training course at work to be precise; a training course that eventually stretched out over many months, and thereby gave us ample opportunity to begin to get to know each other.

Kate, attractive, caring, blond and bubbly; Donna, dark and striking, with a dry, sharp sense of humour; and me.

We enjoyed each other's company, and met together regularly for a gossipy dinner every five or six weeks at one local restaurant or another, or occasionally at one of our houses.

The hitherto loud buzz of conversation from nearby tables in the packed Italian restaurant seemed suddenly to fade into the background, and the evening that had started out in our usual animated, chatty, catching-up kind of way, began to take on an altogether unfamiliar, even sombre feel.

Donna and I were torn between conflicting emotions; pulled one moment into the thrill of the momentous change to come for Kate, and dropped the next into the inevitable sadness of losing her.

I struggled to find the right words, the right questions. There would be no other topic of conversation now – how *could* there be? Kate was leaving us.

I saw my own odd mixture of dismay and delight mirrored on Donna's face.

The beautifully presented fish and pasta dishes that the waiter placed carefully in front of us did not seem quite as appealing as usual, and took us longer to eat, as if we had somehow lost our appetites.

But over the following days the news that Kate, her husband, and the two boys were making plans to emigrate, didn't really sink in with me. I suppose I was, as they say, 'in denial', and from time to time I even caught myself wondering how long it would be before they reversed their decision, and decided not to relocate to the other side of the world after all. Somehow I just didn't think they **would** go.

A whole year passed, and hitch after frustrating hitch glued Kate and her family firmly to the shores of the UK. It was just one difficulty after another, and a never ending procession of seemingly insurmountable obstacles appeared as if by magic between her and the beginning of a bright new life overseas.

Donna and I became used to hearing about the latest problem to beset the would-be travellers, and Kate's attempts to overcome it. We became used to hearing about Australian Visa regulations, astronomical shipping costs, flight fares, and the family's ongoing attempts to secure accommodation in advance of their arrival in Australia.

We listened, and we sympathised as best we could. Actually, we became complacent, and lost sight, I suppose, of the fact that one day Kate would say, "That's *it* Girlies; *we're going*!"

But, after two long years of struggling for what so often seemed unattainable, that is exactly what she said.

The three of us had just sat down at the table in Donna's kitchen, and were contemplating the enticingly chilled bottle of white wine that Donna had opened, and that now stood on the table in front of us.

We stared at Kate.

"Oh my God!" Donna said, "So you're really doing it? You're going?"

Kate nodded. The excitement she felt was written all over her face. A shiny new life finally beckoned, and she was thrilled. Who wouldn't be?

I was lost for words, but smiled and feigned an enthusiasm that, if I'm honest, I did not completely feel. What would we do without our lovely Kate?

My entirely selfish, although perhaps understandable, thoughts obsessed me, and for the next week I could think of little else.

On one of our visits to Kate's house the three of us were sitting chatting in her living room. Soft, early evening sunshine filled the large, pleasant room, and a hint of gentle sea breeze crept in through an open window. I loved Kate's house. It was in the middle of a short row of similar dwellings, right next to the beach. The house itself was attractive, bright, and airy, with spectacular views over the River Mersey and distant Welsh hills.

Suddenly there was a bit of a commotion outside the door that led into the small conservatory attached to the living room, and Kate got up, walked over, and opened the door.

A small, furry missile shot into the room, dragging a thin woollen blanket with him.

"Oh!" I squealed, "Who's this?" laughing as the dog began running round the room, paws skidding noisily on the parquet floor, shaking and growling at the blanket , as if it were a captured rabbit that needed to be subdued.

"Meet Buddy!" Kate said, "probably the biggest character in this house!" and she grinned as the dog raced round her, occasionally tripping, sliding and falling as he stepped on the blanket that dangled from his mouth, and scrabbling to get back up onto his paws again.

Buddy was a Jack Russell. He was small, and basically white, with one or two well defined black patches on his back, and some symmetrical brown marking on his face around the eyes. In short, he was a fairly typical, short coated, long legged Jack Russell.

"Hello!" I called to him as he shot past me, but he completely ignored me and began rolling on his back, kicking his legs in the air and dragging and pulling the blanket over himself.

The little dog's energy was obvious; he was a bundle of fun-seeking activity.

Kate called him, and put him back into the conservatory where, she told us, he spent most of his time, at least during the day while the family were out at work.

106

I had forgotten that Kate had a dog, if indeed I had ever known. I had certainly never met Buddy before.

"You're taking him with you to Australia, are you?" I asked her as she sat back down, wondering how complicated that process of transporting a dog across the world would be, what the regulations were, and how much it would cost.

"We're not sure," Kate said slowly, "we still need to make a decision about that," and her eyes filled with tears – that decision was obviously a potentially heart-breaking one, and I didn't envy her one little bit.

"If you decide not to take him with you," I said, "*we'll* have him. He can come and live with us."

Kate smiled at me, "Thank you," she said, "but if we don't take him we've already promised him to someone else. Sorry."

I felt suddenly, unaccountably disappointed. The little dog had made quite an impression on me. I would have loved to get to know him, to spend time with him.

Once the entry Visas for Australia had been granted to the family arrangements moved pretty fast, and in no time at all a departure date a couple of months away was set, and the one way flights were booked.

Kate and Donna came to our house for lunch, and as they arrived I remember thinking, "I wonder how many more times we'll all be able to meet up? Is *this* maybe the last time?" But I immediately felt guilty, and tried to focus on Kate's happiness, on her wonderful adventure, her new life.

We sat together in the conservatory, enjoying the warmth of the afternoon sun through the glass, catching up on our latest news, looking out at the chickens as they walked about on the grass outside, and laughing as one of them jumped up onto the windowsill and stared in at us, knocking on the window with her beak.

There was a pause in the conversation, and then Kate said, "Fi; you remember Buddy?"

"Course I do," I said.

"Well, we've decided it's best not to take him to Australia with us," Kate said, and her voice broke as the emotion involved in that momentous decision overwhelmed her.

Donna and I waited in silence while Kate took a deep breath and continued.

"You see, he's the sort of dog that chases anything and everything; and he's fast," Kate said. "He's pretty disgusting really, 'cos he catches flies and spiders, and eats them!" She grinned.

"Oh yuck!" we said, pulling faces.

"So I just *know* he'll chase after snakes and crawlies, and try to eat them, and apparently there are plenty of poisonous snakes where we're going." Kate paused, shook her head and sighed, then looked directly at Donna and me, "So," she said quietly, "we think the kindest thing would be to leave him here, in England."

No one spoke. We gazed out the window again, at the garden, the lawn, the greenhouse, the chickens. I wondered idly if there were any snakes out there. I really hoped there weren't.

Donna looked across at Kate.

"Buddy will be fine with your friend. She'll give him a good home," she said kindly, trying to strike a positive note, to cheer Kate up.

"She's decided she can't take him," Kate said, and looked away from us, across the garden, into the distance.

I waited, suddenly hoping, crossing my fingers.

"Do you think *you* could take him Fi?" Kate asked me.

"Oh *yes*! Of course we will!" I said, "We'll look after him Kate, don't you worry!"

I had the oddest mix of sensations – I felt sad for Kate because she was losing a precious, much loved pet, and I knew how difficult that would be for her. But at the same time I was thrilled that Buddy was coming to live with us. I couldn't wait!

A couple of weeks later Donna and I went to Kate's for dinner. Her lovely house, usually so neat and tidy, was in turmoil; of course, why **wouldn't** it be? The family were leaving to go and live abroad - they were voluntarily turning their lives upside down - so turmoil and chaos were the order of the day.

We sat together at the table in the kitchen, amid piles of neatly taped up cardboard boxes, with the pictures missing from the walls, and the ornaments and cooking books gone from the shelves.

We ate dinner off some of the few plates left in the cupboards, using some of the few knives and forks that remained in the house. It was the strangest of times; exciting, thrilling, and oddly depressing.

Buddy had caught the atmosphere, that veritable jumble of feelings and emotions, *of course*. What animal wouldn't? When Kate opened the conservatory door he belted into the living room, raced around, and then shot back to get his blanket. His beloved blanket. We laughed. He ignored me; he couldn't concentrate, couldn't stand still for a moment. I wanted to stroke him, to speak to him, but he was too busy, much too busy.

I would have to wait.

"See you at the weekend!" I told the small, furry missile as we finally drove off, leaving Buddy tucked securely under Kate's arm.

Following the death of my mother a few years previously, my father had moved in with Tod and me. He brought with him, as part of the package, their elderly rescue dog, Misty. She was a small, quiet, sweet tempered old lady, who was happy to just potter about a bit, and sleep a lot. She was a very attractive dog, with a beautiful face and a long, thick coat of almost red fur. She was no trouble at all.

My father had died, but Misty was still with us, and was getting on for fifteen years old. She was very frail, but still sweet, and still pottering about.

Kate was worried that Buddy would be too boisterous and pushy for Misty, that he might accidentally knock her over, and maybe hurt her.

"Take him for a weekend," she said, "and see how they get on together. There's still time to find another home for him if it doesn't work out."

I knew Kate didn't want to 'find another home for him'. I knew that particular scenario would be an emotional nightmare. I hoped we wouldn't have to go there.

Early the next Saturday morning Tod and I drove to Kate's house. She had Buddy's weekend bag packed, and he was wearing his smart collar and lead. He was ready to go. He seemed excited to be going out somewhere, doing something.

Kate led him down the path to our car, and he jumped into the back seat. We drove off quickly, with a minimum of fuss. It was the first time in six years that she had been separated from Buddy. She had had him from a puppy. I felt for her.

I have to admit to feeling nervous as we took Buddy inside our house. We didn't really know him, and had no idea how Misty would react to him either. But we needn't have worried. The two of them got on like a house on fire. They were actually exactly the same height, though Buddy was much stockier than the increasingly frail Misty.

Buddy was, perhaps surprisingly, a perfect gentleman with her, even to the extent of standing back and waiting while Misty ate her dinner, before having his own.

He made himself at home in a gentle, very unassuming kind of way, checking out the rooms in the house, finding the best places to sit, the location of the food bowls, and discovering where we had put his blanket.

There was no squabbling over toys or chews - Buddy always backed down. Misty even permitted him to root through her toy box and take a couple out to play with. We could not have hoped for a friendlier, more peaceful canine relationship!

Peaceful, that is, until we let Buddy into the conservatory and, having jumped up on the chair by the window, he spotted the chickens walking about outside on the lawn.

Now although I would have recognised a Jack Russell if one had passed me on the street, I had never before met one, never spoken to one, never interacted with one. In short, I had no prior knowledge of the character of a Jack Russell.

Buddy had been in our house for a couple of hours, and had shown himself to be a perfectly well-mannered little gentleman. He was courteous with Misty, and did not attempt to grab toys, wolf food or steal chews. Best of all, he didn't rush round spraying the territory! I had already formed the opinion that Buddy was a well brought up little chap.

So it came as a massive shock when this 'well brought up little chap' suddenly erupted like a veritable volcano at the conservatory window.

He didn't just bark or growl at the chickens, oh no, he actually *screamed* at them, producing a kind of high pitched, ear-splitting howl that went on and on. He didn't even seem to take a breath! The shrillness of the noise made our ears ring; it bounced around the conservatory like a barrage of invisible missiles, homing in on us, making any kind of conversation impossible.

He stood up on his back legs, beating at the window with his front paws, *willing* the glass to break, *willing* the window to fall apart and allow him to leap out and grab a chicken, grab *all* the chickens....

111

I was appalled, shocked into immobility, unable to do anything but stare at the 'well brought up little chap' who was acting like a demented Whirling Dervish in front of me.

Tod stepped quickly past me and gathered up the raging fur-ball, tucked him under an arm, and walked out of the conservatory into the back room, carrying the screaming, struggling bundle with him.

"Come in here," he called to me, and I turned, feeling rather dazed, and followed him. Tod pulled the conservatory door closed after me, and put Buddy down on the floor.

The transformation was instant and absolute. We suddenly had our 'well brought up little chap' back again. It was a miracle. Gone was the raging monster of a few minutes before.

I was shaken, and just stared at him as he trotted into the kitchen and had a drink - we heard the slapping of canine tongue on liquid.

Tod and I looked at each other.

"Well…. he'll just have to get used to the chickens," I said slowly, doubtfully, wondering if that would ever happen, "If we let him see them a couple of times a day, maybe…."

"Fo," Tod interrupted me, "Believe me, he will *never* 'get used to them'. He will *always* react like that."

"But surely…." I tried, but couldn't think what else to say. I had never faced a situation like this before.

"It's *in* him. He's that sort of dog," Tod said, "and we either accept that, and work round it, or we can't keep him." He looked at me, waiting for my response, my decision.

I sighed, wondering how easy, or difficult, it would be to keep Buddy away from the chickens; wondering if 'out of sight' *would* actually mean 'out of mind', wondering how much disruption it would cause to our lives; and wondering what would happen if Buddy ever got out into the back garden.

We had sat down in our small back room, Tod on the armchair and me on the sofa next to it. The house was very

112

quiet and peaceful. Misty was asleep upstairs where she spent most of her time these days. She had probably not even heard the commotion – she was getting deaf.

Buddy trotted back in from the kitchen, and with hardly a pause jumped up onto my knee. He stood and stared into my face, just inches away, looking at me, examining me, those big dark eyes getting to know me. I smiled and stroked him along his back, then gave him a kiss on the nose. He suddenly jumped off my knee, walked along the sofa and perched on the arm of the chair, on a level with, and staring straight into Tod's face.

"What do you want then?" Tod asked him gently, reaching out and scratching Buddy's neck. The little dog's stump tail wagged, and he climbed carefully onto Tod's knee and settled down there.

"I think we'll manage, don't you?" Tod said, smiling at me.

"Yes, I think we'll manage very well," I told him, grinning, glad that the right decision had been made.

Shortly after, Tod and Buddy went out for a long walk together. The first of many. They walked along the top of the sea defence wall, that huge grassy mound that runs for miles through a wild, tangled mass of sharp thorned bush and thick undergrowth. Then leaving that high, wind whipped path, they walked down through the quiet shelter of the old woods, the peaceful woods, the woods that have seen the sea level come and go over the years, but which still remain where they had been planted all those years ago.

They came back home two hours later, both of them smiling and happy, both of them pleased to be in each other's company, and both of them considerably muddier than when they went out. A partnership had been born.

That first separation from Buddy was hard for Kate, and we had to take him back to her earlier than planned. She missed him. I knew she would revisit her decision not to take him to

Australia, and I prayed that we would eventually end up with a decision on his future that was right for all concerned.

A couple of weeks later Buddy came to spend another weekend with us. The decision had been made, and this was to be the last 'trial' before he came to live with us permanently. We all came through with flying colours. We simply kept him out of the conservatory - out of sight, and indeed out of mind! We spent the evenings with him in the back room, not in the conservatory.

Buddy and Tod disappeared together for hours at a time, coming back hungry and tired, and happy.

With about a fortnight to go before Kate and her family left the UK, she rang us and suggested that we take Buddy then.

"We haven't got time to spend with him now," she told us, "and he's just sitting here. He's miserable."

So we drove over to Kate's, dreading the finality of the whole thing, dreading seeing Kate's face, dreading taking her dog away from her.

He was packed and waiting for us. Everything was there – towels, blankets, spare collars and lead, bowls, necessary paperwork, shampoo, brush and comb.

Kate gave him a last hug, and bravely walked him down the path to our car. He jumped onto the back seat and she closed the door. The heavy clunk of its closing seemed to underline the finality of the situation. We hugged her, said goodbye, and got into the car. The early morning sun shone down on us.

Kate stood perfectly still in the middle of the quiet, narrow road , watching the car as we drove away, watching Buddy as he stood up at the car's back window and stared out at her. We turned the corner and she was lost to sight.

That image of Kate will forever remain imprinted on my memory. She didn't cry, at least, not in front of us.

But I couldn't stop thinking about her, about how sad she must be feeling at a time when she should be bubbling over with excitement, and looking forward to her new life. A new life without Buddy. *How could she bear it*?

I rang her every day with updates; emailed her with details about how he had settled in with us. Told her he was fine. Told her he was having lots of walks. I felt her pain.

With a week to go Donna and Kate came round to our house for coffee. It was a necessary part of the difficult process of saying goodbye to everyone.

Buddy made a fuss and sat by Kate's feet, looking up at her. We took photos. We didn't know what else to do. When Kate left, Buddy sat at the front door waiting for her to come back again. I felt so sad for them both. Only some of Tod's steak could persuade Buddy to move; quite a lot of Tod's steak actually.

The day we had all been waiting for dawned, and Kate and her family left the UK. I looked at my watch in the early afternoon and knew they had gone. The change had happened, and nothing would ever be the same.

But there *is* a time for everything – that is one of life's certainties.

There is a time for change, a time for coming and going, a time for contemplation, a time for loss, a time for acceptance.

And Buddy had come into our lives as time, that infinite mystery, wrought yet more changes around us. Misty became ill.

Although she tried, she could no longer walk more than a very short distance, and the long treks that Buddy and Tod enjoyed together were out of the question for Misty.

She would potter about our green and pleasantly overgrown large front garden, and then lie down on the grass

115

under the silver birch tree in the middle of the lawn, looking around, sniffing the air. Buddy would sit with her.

Although not in any pain, Misty gradually lost what little vitality she had, and finally we had to carry her up and down stairs, and outside when necessary. She had always had a good appetite, so when she no longer showed any interest in her food, we realised that the end was in sight.

One Saturday morning I carried her to the car, and sat with her on my knee in the back seat as Tod drove us to the Vet's. I cried silently all the way, unable to stop the tears that fell onto the blanket I had wrapped her in.

Buddy had been living with us for two months when we lost Misty.

Two, maybe three weeks later Tod answered a knock at the front door. A delivery driver stood there clutching a parcel for us.

"Sign here please," he said, smiling pleasantly and handing Tod a pen. Tod duly signed for the parcel, reached out and took it from the man.

As he turned to walk off down the path towards his waiting van, the driver looked back over his shoulder and said, "You might want to bring your dog in now, it's starting to rain."

"Err, what dog is that?" Tod asked, confused.

"The little one sitting under the tree," he said, pointing to the silver birch in the middle of the garden, "Pretty little thing, lovely face, almost red fur, isn't it?" And he closed the garden gate behind him, got into his van and drove off, completely unaware, of course, of the immense comfort he had unwittingly provided, or of the fact that the 'pretty little dog' in fact resided in the Spirit World now, and was only revisiting the garden where she had been so happy.

116

Rule one in the Jack Russell handbook of life is that just because you are small it does *not* mean you have to have a small personality. And, as Buddy found himself an only dog, his own particular personality blossomed, and we really got to know the dog beneath the fur.

He was bright, super intelligent, funny, affectionate, and he loved routine.

He doted on Tod and followed him everywhere he could. He very quickly learned that the first walk of the day was at 7am. So, seven in the morning, every day without fail, found Buddy waiting at the front door, stump tail wagging, raring to go.

Back home again after his walk he would have breakfast, and then he'd usually go off to work with Tod. Being self-employed it was pretty easy for Tod to take Buddy with him in his van, and the little dog would sit happily on the passenger seat, staring out through the windscreen, interested in everything he saw. I'd send him off with a couple of biscuits and a chew or two, and his beloved blanket if it was cold.

From time to time Tod couldn't take Buddy with him during the day, so he had to stay at home with me. If I was using the computer Buddy would squeeze onto my knees below the computer table, and stay there, unmoving for hours, waiting for Tod to come back.

I suppose that, in reality, he was probably no different from any number of other bright, intelligent dogs. But to us he very quickly became unique, amazing, a delight, and a massive part of our lives.

We had a good Christmas that year, and Buddy enjoyed his Christmas dinner. He put on weight.

Our early morning routine at home was the same seven days a week. I got up at six, made our breakfast, and got the chickens' breakfast ready. Tod and Buddy would come downstairs in time to go for their walk at 7am.

When they came back an hour, or an hour and a half later, Buddy would race excitedly along the hall straight into the kitchen, skidding on the tiles, and scrabbling to regain his balance. Then he would start on his breakfast, which would be waiting in his bowl.

He loved his breakfast; it was the best meal of the day for him, and he would usually polish it off in no time at all. That always made us laugh.

Then he'd want to play, and would rush off to find his ball.

We loved his enthusiasm, his energy, his fun and affectionate nature. He was bright as a button. What had we ever done without him?

It was simply a fleeting thought at first. Not even a fully formed thought really, more of a feather-light whisper in my mind. It did not enter my consciousness, but played around on the surface, at the edges.

It remained there for a couple of days, almost grasped, almost articulated, but not quite.

Then one day Tod came in and said, "He was sick this morning."

And I felt a pressure at the back of my neck, like fingers gently touching me.

Buddy sniffed at his breakfast, and walked away from it. He settled down on the sofa in the back room, and went to sleep. We watched him.

"Is he ok?" I asked Tod anxiously.

"Oh yes; he's probably eaten something he found outside. That nose is a radar for anything edible. He'll sleep it off," Tod said, "Don't worry."

But I did.

Buddy slept most of the day. I sat with him from time to time and spoke to him, stroked him. He leapt off the sofa when Tod came in that evening, and jumped around him, wanting a walk.

"He probably needs one," I said, "he's been asleep most of the day. But he seems better now. Better than he was."

The next morning Buddy was back to his normal boisterous self. He enjoyed his walk as usual, dashing about with the other dogs, but was sick in the kitchen when he came back. He didn't touch his breakfast, didn't even sniff at it, and curled up on the sofa and went to sleep.

I looked at him and those fingers touched the back of my neck again. I shivered. A dull, heavy feeling of impending panic began to creep down my spine. What *was* it I had noticed about Buddy recently? There was something different. Something not quite right. *What*?

I stood by the sofa and looked down at him sleeping, that precious little creature, and suddenly realised that he had lost weight. Yes, he *had* lost weight. Quite a lot of weight.

Not so very long ago he had been chubby – we had even talked about a diet for him, but because he was so active we had not yet implemented one, reasoning that exercise would probably regulate his weight, and a diet would not be needed.

It was Saturday. We bought fresh chicken pieces and tried to tempt Buddy to eat that evening. He sat on Tod's knee, his usual evening position, and accepted a couple of pieces. Not much.

But then he wanted to play, and ran off to get his ball, barking and racing through the kitchen after it as Tod threw it for him. We laughed. We loved seeing him enjoying himself.

But I could not shake off that feeling of anxiety that verged on panic. It hovered over me, threatening to close in.

"We'll take him to the Vet on Monday," I said, "Have him checked over. Just to be sure he's ok."

But he *wasn't* ok. We knew it. We felt it. We dreaded it.

When he came back from his walk the next morning he simply walked slowly through the kitchen, head down, not even stopping to look at his bowl, or at me, and lay down on

119

the carpet in the back room. He didn't attempt to jump up onto the sofa.

Tod shook his head.

"It's strange," he said quietly, looking down at Buddy, "he's been ok, running round with the other dogs, jumping about with them as usual."

Buddy stood up and was sick on the carpet.

I phoned our Vets. They hold a surgery on a Sunday morning in a village about a thirty minute drive away from home.

Buddy lay completely still on the back seat of the car as we drove off. His usual agitated nosiness that always made us laugh so much, as he rushed from window to window, staring out, watching other cars go by, barking at people, was gone. He didn't move.

It was summertime, July to be exact.

We drove through a beautiful north of England countryside made more beautiful by flourishing greenery and ripening crops. The air was warm and fresh, and carried in it the fragrance of a thousand blossoming summer flowers.

Surely nothing bad could ever happen on a wonderful day like this, could it?

I stared straight ahead, not interested in the scenery around me. I glanced at Tod and noticed how pale he looked, how solemn. We drove in silence, consumed by our own anxious thoughts.

Our Vets are kind and caring, and we have a great deal of confidence in them. We are lucky.

Tod lifted Buddy onto the table in the surgery, keeping one hand on his back to reassure him. Buddy stood quietly, head down. We explained his symptoms, and the Vet examined him carefully, expertly, "There seems to be some kind of mass in the abdomen," he said quietly after a moment. "An x ray will show us more. Can you leave him with us? I'll be as quick as possible."

We agreed. The Vet said he would ring us later that day with the results. We waited while a nurse took Buddy away, walking him out of the surgery into the rooms at the back, where he would have the x-ray. Buddy glanced at us, and then slowly followed her.

We left.

"He'll be alright," Tod said as we got into the car outside the surgery, "He'll be alright."

I couldn't speak. I didn't dare speak. There were too many tears waiting. We drove back home in silence.

It was the longest Sunday I can ever remember. Time stood still.

Tod went outside and chopped wood. I used to love the sound of his axe splitting the logs, but on that day it sounded strange, somehow disagreeable and unpleasant.

The sun shone. It was warm. The local cricket team started a match on the field behind our house. How could they shout? How could they laugh? I wanted to go outside and tell them to go somewhere else, to leave us alone, and to give us some peace while we waited.

I sat in the conservatory staring out at the garden, seeing nothing.

Some time later the Vet rang. He told us that the x ray showed there was indeed a mass in Buddy's abdomen, a very large mass. A tumour.

An operation was the only realistic way of examining this growth, he said, and of deciding how best to proceed with treatment.

"Will you be able to remove it?" I asked croakily. My mouth had dried up, and my voice was little short of a rasp.

"I won't know until I see it," the Vet said, "but try not to worry."

But worry we did. Of course.

He wanted to operate on Buddy as soon as possible, probably later that same afternoon. I told Tod. He looked at me and said nothing. What was there to say?

It was hot in the conservatory, so I went into the back room and sat down on the sofa. I leant back against the cushions and closed my eyes.

My hand encountered something soft. Buddy's blanket. His blanket. He would need it. He would want it. Why hadn't we taken it to the Vet's with him earlier?

Tod came in and sat down beside me.

"This just can't be happening," I said, "What if we lose him?" and that feeling, that awful feeling of impending panic that had been hanging over me for so long began to close in, to take hold of me.

"Come on," Tod said, and he stood up. "We'll go and see him before he has the operation."

I grabbed Buddy's blanket, and followed Tod quickly out of the house. It felt better to be doing something, to have a purpose.

We drove again through the early summer countryside, past the beautiful cottage we had wanted to buy but couldn't afford, past the field where the rescued donkeys lived happily, past the swathe of swaying, ripening wheat in the field with the old stone wall round it, past the animal sanctuary where Tod had helped out, and back into the lovely old village of Rufford.

The young nurse in the Vet's understood; she was gentle, caring, and pretended not to notice my tears.

"I'll get him for you," she said. "He's a bit dopey from the pre-med, but you can sit with him in here," and she opened the door to a private room, and showed us in.

A few moments later she came back. She was carrying Buddy. As soon as he saw us he started to struggle, wanting down, wanting to see us.

"Why don't you sit down," the nurse said to Tod, "and I'll pass him to you."

Buddy settled down on Tod's knee. I put his blanket over him and kissed him on the top of his head. He wagged his stump and settled himself more comfortably. He tried to keep his eyes open, to stay awake, but in a few moments he was asleep.

We sat with him for an hour. Every so often he would wake up, lift his head, see that we were still there, and go back to sleep.

Eventually the nurse came for him, and Tod passed Buddy to her with his blanket.

"Try not to worry," she said kindly, "the Vet may be able to remove it, you know."

We both kissed Buddy, told him we'd see him later, and stumbled out of the surgery into the narrow road outside, with the lovely olde worlde houses and ancient stone walls along it. Summer birdsong filled the bright air, the leaves on the trees rustled above us, and the voices of the sheep in the adjacent field reached us on the warm breeze.

I looked up at the clear blue sky above, and prayed that we wouldn't lose him.

I cried all the way home. Looking back, I suppose I knew. I had known for some time.

Tod and I sat in the conservatory. It was late afternoon and the air was cooler. We sat in uneasy silence and looked out at the garden, watched the chickens. Waited.

Tod answered the phone at 7.30pm that evening.

The massive tumour was firmly attached to several of the major organs, and was already pressing on them, causing severe discomfort. The Vet could not remove it.

And so we lost him. We lost Buddy.

He took away with him part of our lives, and a piece of our hearts.

He left behind him a wealth of happy memories.

Buddy had shared, and enhanced our lives for a year. Just one year. We are so very grateful that he did.

I came downstairs in the early morning light, shortly after that awful, black day, and began tidying up in the kitchen. All done, I opened the back room door and walked in, meaning to open up the conservatory and let the day's already warm air into the house.

But I stopped in mid stride, my hand still on the door handle, staring.

There in the middle of the carpet lay Buddy's blanket, all scrunched up, just as if he had been playing with it and left it there, as he had done so many times. But I knew I had washed it the day before, and hung it on the line in the outhouse. It should still have been there.

Some time later, maybe a month, Tod and I came home from shopping. Having sorted the purchases out in the kitchen, I walked through the hall to the bottom of the stairs, carrying several items destined for the bathroom shelves. My foot was hardly on the first stair when I heard a sound from above and looked up, wondering what it was. There, standing together, side by side on the landing, looking down the stairs towards me, were Misty and Buddy. Although their forms were somewhat hazy, as if I was seeing them through a moving cloud of smoke or mist of varying density, I could see their tails wagging as they watched me.

I was thrilled, elated, as I always am when I am privileged to see a visitor from the Spirit World. But this particular visitation was something very special, and I simply cannot put into words how wonderful that moment was. It actually *was* just a moment though, and then the dogs gradually faded from my view, back into another dimension.

I called to Tod and told him what I had seen. We sat together on the bottom stair, arms round each other, both of us damp eyed and emotional, talking, laughing, and remembering our much loved canine friends, as they had remembered us.

"You think dogs will not be in heaven? I tell you, they will be there long before any of us."
Robert Louis Stevenson.

Chapter Fifteen

Andrew

My friend Ruth could best be described as healthily sceptical where anything to do with Spiritualism, the Paranormal, and mediumship are concerned. And that, of course, is no bad thing.

However, one day I found myself round at Ruth's house having a cup of coffee and doing a private reading for her, for the very first time.

Although I remember that we laughed a lot for an hour or so, most of the actual content of the reading is now lost in the mists of time, except, that is, for the very last part of it, because just as I was bringing the reading to a close I heard a voice shout, "Andrew" from the Spirit World. It was just that one name, unaccompanied by any other information, or any other sound, except loud and prolonged laughter.

When I asked her, the name 'Andrew' didn't mean anything in particular to Ruth. There was no one close to her with that name, she didn't work with an 'Andrew', or even have an acquaintance called 'Andrew'. We drew a blank.

But the name was called out again, and again it was accompanied by loud laughter.

"There must be *some* significance," I said, "however trivial; so maybe just keep an eye open for any Andrews in the vicinity!" We both laughed. There was nothing else to do. The identity of 'Andrew' remained a mystery.

A week later Ruth and her daughter Alice went shopping to the local supermarket. They drove there, and having completed their shop, they loaded it into the car boot and began the short drive home again.

Dusk was falling as they turned into their narrow, pleasant road, but the street lights had not yet come on. Long dark shadows crept across in front of the car, and visibility was somewhat reduced.

Suddenly Alice said, "Stop Mum! Stop! There's someone lying on the pavement over there," and she twisted round in the seat and pointed across the road at a spot which they had already driven past.

Ruth pulled the car up. The road was quiet with no other traffic about at that time of the evening. They both looked over, squinting through the fading light to see what it was on the pavement behind them.

"Alice, are you sure it's a person?" Ruth said. "From here it just looks like a pile of rubbish someone has dumped there."

"I'm sure!" Alice told her, "It's someone lying there. They must be ill," and so saying she opened the door and started to get out of the car.

"Wait a minute," Ruth said, "Wait for me," and she switched the engine off and also got out of the car.

They crossed the road together and walked quickly along towards the unknown object on the pavement. As they drew closer they could both see that it was indeed a body, and it wasn't moving.

It was a man of maybe early middle age, and he was unconscious. He seemed to have either fallen and banged his head on the pavement, or he had been attacked, because there was blood on his face.

While Alice used her mobile to call an ambulance Ruth crouched down beside the man and was immediately enveloped in a very strong smell of alcohol that hung around him like an invisible cloud.

"Oh dear," she thought, "It looks like he's drunk."

A short time later the ambulance arrived. The medics checked the man over and then lifted him onto a stretcher and put him in the back of the ambulance.

Ruth and Alice had stood silently, watching and waiting, while the medics did their job, but now Ruth approached one of them and asked, "Will he be alright?"

"Do you know him?" the medic asked her.

"No," she said. "We just found him lying here on the pavement."

"Well," the man said, shaking his head, "this isn't the first time we've been called out to pick him up off the pavement!" And he smiled ruefully. "Chances are it won't be the last. He has an alcohol problem."

"The poor man," Ruth said, "I'll ring the hospital later to see how he's getting on," and she and Alice started to walk away, back towards the car.

"Oh! I forgot," she said, stopping suddenly and turning back towards the medic who was just closing the ambulance doors, "Do you know what his name is?"

"Andrew," the medic called to her, "his name's Andrew."

Ruth rang me later that day and told me what had happened.

"Explain!" she said, "What's the significance of all this? I mean, why did the Spirit World tell us that poor man's name? What's that all about?"

"Well, you probably won't like this," I said, "in fact, I **know** you won't like this, but…. I don't know! So I can't answer your question with any certainty, I'm afraid, but I **can** try and make an informed guess."

"Huh! Well go on then, do your best!" my friend said. "Guess away!"

I laughed.

"My best guess would be that this has got your attention," I said. "You're interested, you want to know what's going on, and you have maybe moved a small step closer to a belief in the existence of the Spirit World, and the fact that there is no such actual state as 'death'. Life goes on across the divide, but in a different way. And as has just been demonstrated, those in the Spirit World are able to look a short distance into our future. I think that they have used that ability here to tap you on the shoulder, and to get you thinking!"

"Huh!" Ruth said.

I laughed. I am very fond of my friend Ruth!

"The day which we fear as our last is but the birthday of eternity."
Seneca.

129

Thank you for taking the time to read this book. I hope its contents have, at the very least, given you pause for thought.

It is easy to look around at the world we live in today, and feel despair, anguish, and hopelessness. For intolerance, violence, mistrust, and a pressing desire to dominate the thoughts, beliefs, and lives of our fellow man, seem to have overtaken, even obliterated, peace, kindness and compassion in so many regions.

You will perhaps forgive me for reproducing here some of my very favourite quotations. They seem particularly apt in this current wretched and uncertain epoch.

"I shall pass this way but once; any good that I can do, or any kindness I can show to any human being, let me do it now. Let me not defer nor neglect it, for I shall not pass this way again."
Etienne de Grellet, Quaker Missionary.

"Be the change that you wish to see in the world."
Mahatma Gandhi

"If you want others to be happy, practice compassion. If you want to be happy, practice compassion."
Dalai Lama

"Walk cheerfully over the world answering that of God in everyone."
1656. George Fox. Religious Society of Friends.

For details on all books by Fiona Roberts please see
www.spanglefish.com/fionaroberts

Made in the USA
Charleston, SC
02 September 2016